TORONTO EATS

BESTSELLING AUTHOR OF
TORONTO COOKS

AMY ROSEN

TORONTO EATS

100

SIGNATURE RECIPES

FROM THE

CITY'S BEST

RESTAURANTS

Figure 1
Vancouver / Berkeley

Cataloguing data is available from Library and Archives Canada
ISBN 978-1-77327-003-6 (hbk.)

Design by Jessica Sullivan
Photography by Ryan Szulc, www.ryanszulc.ca
Prop styling by Madeleine Johari
Photography assistance by Matt Gibson and Alex Knabenschuh

Editing by Michelle Meade
Copy editing by Linda Pruessen
Proofreading by Renate Preuss
Indexing by Jane Broderick

Printed and bound in China by C&C Offset Printing Co.
Distributed in the U.S. by Publishers Group West

Figure 1 Publishing Inc.
Vancouver BC Canada
www.figure1publishing.com

To all of the hardworking chefs, cooks, front and back-of-house staff, farmers, bakers, cheesemakers, winemakers, and chocolatiers who create the experiences that make Toronto such a wonderful place to live. And to my family and friends, who make this big city feel like home.

CONTENTS

Introduction

A LOT CAN HAPPEN IN A COUPLE OF YEARS.
Little did we know, when we last met, that *Toronto Cooks*, a cookbook celebrating the culinary landscape of the city, was about to become the little book that could. It shot to the top five cookbooks on Amazon over Christmas of 2014, nestled snugly between Ina Garten and Jamie Oliver (that's a sandwich I'll never get sick of). Indigo stores erected six-foot-tall *Toronto Cooks* book trees, while independent shops such as Type Books and Labour of Love faithfully restocked their stacks each morning. I am grateful to them, grateful to the readers, and most of all grateful to the chefs who took a chance and honoured us all with their recipes and histories.

Now we're back for seconds, and this time, our shining city by the lake has come even further in its dining evolution without forgoing its past.

With more than 100 recipes from 50 amazing chefs, several of whom were featured in the first book, *Toronto Eats* documents this progression. Our city's chefs represent the countless cultures, and their flavours and techniques, that make up the culinary fabric of our city today. From Mumbai chili crab (page 114) to okonomiyaki (page 111), the world appears on our dinner plates.

The farms, forests, and lakes that surround us give us local and sustainable ingredients and a good bit of foraging too. Think wood-nettle spätzle (page 39) or slow-cooked chicken with fresh corn pudding (page 98). We're a city that likes to cheer on our sports teams with one-handed party food (the other hand needed for fist-pumping and beer-drinking), and that's where homemade pizzas (pages 135, 165), fried chicken (page 213), and fish tacos (page 106) come in handy.

But we also like to have a healthy balance in our lives, so say hello to pear and parsnip soup (page 17), turkey chili (page 85), vegan zucchini manicotti (page 127), and black bean and sweet potato tacos (page 68). That said, we also have a major sweet tooth and love getting high on chocolate chip cookie squares (page 181), brownies (page 90), and banana cream pie éclairs (page 184).

We are a city on the rise. Here, a new generation of chefs—who have learned well from generous mentors—have opened their own spots, where they whip up everything from choucroute garnie (page 191) to beef tartare (page 32). But our culinary originators are still very much in the game, and continue to push the restaurant industry further. *Toronto Eats* is a gorgeous illustration of this city's food scene, featuring chef-tested recipes from our most talented toques, as well as their stories. With the reader in mind, it's designed to make favourite restaurant dishes, including all of those mentioned above, achievable for the eager home cook. It's also a reminder of how lucky we are to live in this city.

And it's because of those who came before, and because of those arriving daily with fresh dreams, that we are Toronto the Delicious.

THE RECIPES

Appetizers

Soups and Salads

Drinks

Mains

Sides

Desserts

Art Gallery of Ontario
Renée Bellefeuille

THE ART GALLERY OF ONTARIO'S FRANK restaurant is a distinctly Frank Gehry–designed space. Its casually curved décor is a wash of blond wood, modern Danish furnishings, and sunlight, and on any given day, the place is filled with chatter as gallery-goers tuck into brunches of Basque-style eggs while polishing off a bottle of Norman Hardie unfiltered chardonnay. Executive chef Renée Bellefeuille—who's worked at the Drake Hotel, the Consulate General of France in Toronto, and as Jamie Kennedy's pastry chef—takes inspiration from around the globe and right in her own backyard. The two recipes she's contributed to this book—a herbaceous spatchcocked hen with fresh corn polenta and tomato jam, and a cashew-pandan mousse with passion fruit purée—embrace our town's cultural diversity. "Toronto is a city with so many flavours at our fingertips, and using those flavours combined with more traditional preparations is how I think about creating menus throughout the gallery," she says. Bellefeuille is also responsible for the menus at caféAGO, the Espresso Bar in the Galleria Italia, and the Norma Ridley Members' Lounge, and under her guidance, the gallery has become a culinary hub of sorts. "It's important for me to show skills that are from the savoury and the sweet kitchen, as both areas are of equal joy to me."

FACING: Spatchcocked Cornish Hen, Honey Herb and Spice Butter, Fresh Corn Polenta, and Tomato Jam

Honey herb and spice butter

1 cup unsalted butter, softened
½ bunch fresh marjoram, finely chopped
2 Tbsp wildflower honey
1½ tsp kosher salt
1 tsp chili flakes
½ tsp ground fennel seeds, toasted
½ tsp ground coriander, toasted
Zest of 2 lemons

Cornish hen

2 cups brown sugar, packed
2 bay leaves
5 Tbsp kosher salt
1 tsp star anise
1 tsp cardamom pods
4 cups boiling water

4 cups ice-cold water
2 Cornish hens (1½ lbs each),
   backbones removed by butcher
Vegetable oil, for brushing
2 Tbsp extra-virgin olive oil
Salt and freshly ground black pepper

 Serves 4–6

Spatchcocked Cornish Hen, Honey Herb and Spice Butter, Fresh Corn Polenta, and Tomato Jam

Honey herb and spice butter Place butter in the bowl of a stand mixer fitted with a paddle attachment and beat for 1 minute to aerate. Add remaining ingredients and beat for another 1½ minutes. Using a rubber spatula, scrape down the sides of the mixing bowl and beat for 30 seconds. Scrape butter into a lidded container and set aside (or refrigerate until later use).

Cornish hen To a bowl or pot large enough to hold the water and the Cornish hens, add all dry ingredients and pour in the boiling water. Stir until sugar and salt have dissolved.

Add ice water to the bowl, stir, and refrigerate for 2 hours or until mixture has chilled. Add Cornish hens and refrigerate, covered, for another 8 to 12 hours.

Preheat a clean barbecue grill over a medium flame and brush the grill with vegetable oil. Transfer hens to a cutting board and pat dry with paper towels. Rub hens with olive oil and sprinkle with salt and pepper. Place hens on the side of the grill without the flame, skin-side down. Close the lid and cook for 20 minutes. Rotate hens 90 degrees, close lid, and cook for another 5 to 10 minutes, or until the internal temperature reaches 170°F. Transfer hens to a platter and brush liberally with honey herb and spice butter. Set aside to rest while you prepare the tomato jam.

Tomato jam

5 ripe heirloom tomatoes
  (approx. 2 lbs), finely chopped
2 small cooking onions, finely chopped
2 cups cane sugar
1 cup chardonnay white wine vinegar
1 Tbsp yellow mustard seeds
2 tsp nigella seeds

Polenta

6 ears of corn
2¼ cups water, divided
5 Tbsp unsalted butter, divided
1 small cooking onion, finely diced
¼ tsp salt
Freshly ground black pepper
7 oz goat cheese, crumbled

Tomato jam In a medium saucepan, combine all ingredients and bring to a boil on high heat. Reduce heat to medium-low and simmer for 1½ hours, stirring occasionally to prevent jam from sticking to the pan. Spoon into a small bowl and reserve until dinner.

Polenta Remove the leaves and silk from each ear of corn, then chop off the pointed top and stalk. Using a sharp knife, shave off kernels, then place them in a medium saucepan and add enough water to cover. Bring to a gentle simmer and cook for 15 minutes. Strain off the corn, reserving the liquid. Add corn to a food processor and pulse, adding 1½ cups water (or as needed) to purée.

To the same saucepan, add 3 Tbsp butter and the onions and cook on low heat for 15 minutes, until lightly caramelized. Add corn purée, salt and pepper, and any remaining water, stirring for 10 to 15 minutes, or until mixture thickens to a mashed potato consistency.

Fold in remaining 2 Tbsp butter, goat cheese, and salt to taste. Serve immediately. This family-style meal can be served in separate dishes to be passed around the table.

Pandan syrup

12 fresh pandan leaves
1 cup granulated sugar
½ cup water

Cashew-pandan butter

2½ cups unsalted cashews
¼ cup hot water, plus extra as needed
2 Tbsp canola oil
1 cup Pandan Syrup (see here)

Mousse

4 egg yolks
1 tsp vanilla paste
4 Tbsp granulated sugar, divided
3 leaves gelatin
¼ cup white rum
¾ cup Cashew-Pandan Butter
  (see here)
2 cups whipping (35%) cream

Passion fruit purée

1 cup frozen passion fruit
  concentrate
¼ cup granulated sugar,
  plus extra as needed

 Serves 4

Cashew-Pandan Mousse, Passion Fruit Purée, and Lime Tuile

Pandan syrup Using the back of a knife, bruise pandan leaves. In a small pot, combine all ingredients and cook on medium-low heat for 10 minutes, until sugar is dissolved. Set aside to cool. Refrigerate and allow to steep overnight. Strain, reserving syrup.

Cashew-pandan butter Preheat the oven to 325°F. Place cashews on a parchment-lined baking sheet and roast for 10 to 12 minutes, or until golden brown. Set aside 1 cup for use in Spiced Cashews recipe (on facing page).

Combine all ingredients in a blender or food processor and purée until smooth. (Add additional hot water by the tablespoon, if needed, until a smooth paste is formed.) Set aside at room temperature.

Mousse In a double boiler, combine egg yolks, vanilla paste, and 2 Tbsp sugar and whisk continuously over medium heat until mixture makes thick ribbons when dropped from a spoon. This is your sabayon.

Soak gelatin in a bowl of cold water until dissolved. Place rum in a small saucepan on low heat. Squeeze excess water from gelatin, add to saucepan, and mix well until gelatin has dissolved. Stir mixture into sabayon.

Place cashew-pandan butter into a medium bowl and whisk in an eighth of the sabayon. Fold in remaining sabayon.

In a separate bowl, whip cream with the remaining 2 Tbsp of sugar until stiff peaks form. Fold half of the whipped cream into the butter mixture, and then add remaining cream. Transfer to a sealable container and refrigerate for 4 hours or overnight to set.

Passion fruit purée In a small saucepan on medium heat, simmer passion fruit concentrate for 30 minutes, until reduced by half. Stir in sugar and adjust sweetness to taste. Set aside to cool and chill until needed.

Lime tuile

½ cup unsalted butter, softened
1 cup icing sugar, sifted
Zest of 3 limes
4 egg whites
½ tsp vanilla extract
½ cup all-purpose flour
Salt

Spiced cashews

2 Tbsp granulated sugar
1 Tbsp water
5 Tbsp unsalted butter, divided
1 cup toasted cashews (reserved from
    Cashew-Pandan Butter recipe)
Pinch cayenne
Pinch chili powder
¼ tsp chili flakes
Salt

Assembly

Icing sugar, for dusting

To make the classic tuile shape, lay the hot cookie on a rolling pin, juice bottle, or small can (any heat-proof object can serve as a mould). The tuile will firm up in 1 minute and should release easily.

Lime tuile Preheat the oven to 300°F. Line a baking sheet with a non-stick baking mat.

In the bowl of a stand mixer fitted with paddle attachment, cream together butter, icing sugar, and lime zest for 5 minutes. Add half of the egg whites, and the vanilla extract, scraping down the sides of the bowl with a rubber spatula. Add remaining 2 egg whites and mix well. Add flour and a pinch of salt, mixing until just combined. Scrape down the sides of the bowl and mix again for another minute. Chill for 1 hour.

Line a baking sheet with parchment paper and spray liberally with non-stick spray. (Alternatively, line the baking sheet with a non-stick baking mat.) Spoon a small amount of tuile batter onto the baking sheet. Using an offset spatula, spread batter as evenly and thinly as possible into a circle or your desired shape.

Bake for 9 to 10 minutes, until golden. Remove the pan from the oven and immediately (and carefully) slide a spatula under the edge of the cookie. After 10 seconds or so, the shape will hold and the tuile will slide off the sheet with the spatula. Work quickly to complete all tuiles. Allow to cool and place in a sealed airtight container until ready to assemble.

Spiced cashews In a small saucepan on medium heat, combine sugar, water, and 2 Tbsp butter.

In a medium ovenproof bowl, melt the remaining 3 Tbsp of butter. Add cashews, spices, and butter syrup. Toss and adjust seasoning to taste. Pour onto a parchment-lined baking sheet and set aside to cool.

To assemble Place a scoop of mousse in the centre of a wide, shallow bowl. Drizzle passion fruit purée around the mousse. Wedge 2 to 3 tuiles into the base of the mousse and sprinkle with spiced cashews. Dust with icing sugar. Repeat with remaining serving bowls and enjoy.

Ascari Enoteca

John Sinopoli

IN THE HEART of Leslieville sits a jumpin' neighbourhood pasta and wine bar where chef and co-owner John Sinopoli (along with Erik Joyal) has reimagined a yoga studio into a 38-seat restaurant with an open kitchen, fishbowl windows, friendly greetings, and a progressive wine list. "We're extremely heavy on biodynamic and natural wines," says Sinopoli. "We call them wines with soul." They all have a story to tell, as does the food, which includes handmade pastas and sharable appetizers like the ethereal broccolini fritti, and crostini *al tonno conserva* (olive oil–poached albacore tuna on smashed navy beans atop fried bread). "It's a perfect two-bite snack when drinking a glass of white wine," says Sinopoli of this popular starter.

Other dishes on the menu taste just like they do at your imaginary Italian grandma's on Sunday (think Stracci con Salsiccia, a house-made pork sausage with fresh pasta "rags"). And then there are dishes that your imaginary nonna would never serve but would love nonetheless (pasta tossed with saffron-braised chicken, artichokes, and olives). Drinking and dining at Ascari Enoteca is as heartwarming as a pot of tomato sauce bubbling away on the Sunday stovetop.

FACING: Crostini al Tonno Conserva

Tuna conserva
4 cups olive oil
4 sprigs fresh rosemary
3 cloves garlic
2 fresh bay leaves
1 (1-inch-wide) strip of
   lemon peel
6 oz Albacore tuna loin,
   cut into 3 pieces

Pickled onion
1 cup white wine vinegar
1 cup water
¼ cup granulated sugar
1 Tbsp kosher salt
1 red onion, thinly sliced
   into rounds

Braised beans
1 cup dried navy beans
1 white onion, halved
1 carrot, peeled and halved
1 rib celery, halved
1 sprig fresh rosemary
2 Tbsp salt, plus extra to taste
Freshly ground black pepper
2 (1-inch-wide) strips
   lemon zest

 **Makes 9 crostini**

Crostini al Tonno Conserva

Tuna conserva In a medium saucepan on medium heat, combine olive oil, rosemary, garlic, bay leaves, and lemon peel and heat mixture to 160°F (use a candy thermometer to measure temperature). Remove the pan from the heat, add tuna, and set aside to cool. Refrigerate, covered, until ready to use. Remove from the fridge and bring to room temperature 30 minutes before assembly.

Pickled onion Combine vinegar, water, sugar, and salt in a saucepan, bring to a boil on high heat, and cook for 2 to 3 minutes, or until sugar has dissolved.

Place onions in a glass bowl, pour in pickling liquid, and set aside to cool, then refrigerate. Onions are best if pickled for 24 hours, and can be kept covered in the fridge for several days.

Braised beans Combine beans and 8 cups of water in a large bowl and soak overnight. Drain, place beans in a medium pot, and add enough fresh water to cover beans by 2 to 3 inches. Add onions, carrots, celery, rosemary, and salt and bring to a boil on high heat. Reduce heat to medium-low and simmer gently for 60 to 90 minutes, until beans are tender and creamy. (Skim off any foam or scum that rises to the top.) Season with salt and pepper to taste. Add lemon strips. Remove beans from the heat and set aside to cool. Refrigerate until needed.

Anchovy vinaigrette

2 canned anchovies

¼ cup red wine vinegar

1 Tbsp Pickled Onions (see here)

1 tsp Dijon mustard

2 cups extra-virgin olive oil

Salt and freshly ground
  black pepper

Assembly

½ sourdough baguette (or 1 ficelle)

¼ cup olive oil

¼ bunch chives, finely chopped

Blanched broccolini stems, chopped,
  or sliced green beans, to serve
  (optional)

Anchovy vinaigrette Combine anchovies, vinegar, onions, and mustard in a blender and blend until smooth. Gradually add olive oil in a steady stream and season with salt and pepper to taste.

To assemble Cut baguette diagonally, about ¼ inch thick and 3 inches long (9 slices in total). Heat olive oil in a frying pan on medium-low, add baguette slices, and fry for 20 to 30 seconds, or until golden. Flip over and fry for another 20 to 30 seconds.

Drain beans and transfer 1 cup of beans to a medium bowl. Mash beans with a fork so that about half are a paste. Add 2 Tbsp anchovy vinaigrette and stir to loosen the beans. Spoon bean mixture onto a fried baguette slice and use the back of a spoon to gently flatten. Repeat with remaining pieces and place on a serving platter.

Break up each piece of poached tuna into 3 chunks. Top each crostini with a piece of tuna and garnish with pickled onion and chives. Serve with chopped broccolini stems or sliced green beans, if using.

Pasta

3¼ cups (400 g) "00" flour, plus extra for dusting (see Tip)

⅔ cup (100 g) semolina, plus extra for consistency, if needed

3 whole eggs

7 egg yolks

Tomato sauce

6 Tbsp extra-virgin olive oil

½ large white onion, halved and thinly sliced

2 cloves garlic, thinly sliced

1 red pepper, halved and seeded

3 cans (28 oz each) San Marzano or good-quality whole tomatoes, hand-crushed with their liquid

Salt and freshly ground black pepper

3 basil leaves, torn

All-purpose flour will work but "00" flour results in a more delicate and tender noodle. You can find "00" flour in many Italian supermarkets or specialty baking stores.

 Serves 4

Stracci con Salsiccia

Pasta Sift flours together onto a clean surface and make a well in the centre. Pour eggs and yolks into the well and gently beat with a fork, slowly incorporating the flour from the inside edge of the well into the eggs and mixing until it forms a thick paste. Using a pastry scraper, fold the rest of the flour into the mixture to form a dough. Fold dough onto itself and knead until dough just comes together in one piece and has a smooth surface (do not overwork).

Place dough on a well-floured surface, wrap loosely with plastic wrap, and rest for at least 1 hour. Roll out dough through a pasta roller, reducing the thickness one setting at a time (this avoids stressing the dough) until it's the thickness of a nickel (coin). Generously sprinkle flour onto a tray and lay pasta on top, then cover loosely with plastic wrap and let rest for another 10 to 15 minutes.

Return the sheets to a lightly floured work surface and, using a large knife or a fluted pasta cutter wheel, cut into 1½ × 4-inch strips. Line a baking sheet with parchment paper and sprinkle with semolina. Lay your *stracci* ("rags") on top, making sure they do not overlap. Place in the freezer for 3 hours, or until frozen.

Once frozen, place 22 oz of stracci in a sealed container and return to the freezer until ready to use. If there is extra, freeze in a separate container for future use (it will keep for several months).

Tomato sauce Heat olive oil in a large pot on medium-high. Add onions and sauté until soft and translucent, about 7 minutes. Add garlic and sauté for another minute, until fragrant. Add red pepper, tomatoes, salt, and pepper. Reduce heat to medium-low and simmer uncovered for 45 to 60 minutes, stirring occasionally. Adjust seasoning to taste. Add basil, remove from the heat, and allow to cool. Set aside.

Peperonata

2 Tbsp olive oil

1 large white onion, halved and thinly sliced

1 clove garlic, thinly sliced

Salt and freshly ground black pepper

2 red peppers, seeded and sliced into ¼-inch strips

2 orange peppers, seeded and sliced into ¼-inch strips

2 yellow peppers, seeded and sliced into ¼-inch strips

2 sprigs fresh rosemary

Assembly

8 oz fennel and pork sausage

¼ cup canola oil

½ fennel bulb, separated into layers and cut into 1-inch dice

1 cup Peperonata (see here)

1½ cups Tomato Sauce (see here)

Fennel fronds, for garnish

Pinch of sea salt

Do your best to source good-quality sausage from a butcher that makes their own using quality pork and as little nitrate as possible. Sinopoli has used fennel and pork sausage, but this dish is also fantastic with a bit of chili. Any leftover tomato sauce or peperonata can be stored for up to 10 days in the fridge.

Peperonata Heat olive oil in a large frying pan on medium. Add onions and sauté for 7 minutes, until translucent. Add garlic and cook for another minute, until fragrant. Season with salt and pepper.

Add peppers and rosemary, stir, and cook for another 10 to 15 minutes, until the peppers are done (but not mushy). Check seasoning and adjust with salt and pepper, if needed. Remove rosemary and set aside to cool.

To assemble Remove sausage from its casing and break into large chunks. Heat canola oil in a large frying pan on medium-high. Add sausage and sauté for 5 minutes, until just cooked through. Using a slotted spoon, transfer sausage to a plate lined with paper towel and set aside.

To the same pan, add fennel and cook until golden brown, about 7 to 10 minutes. Return sausage to the pan, add peperonata with all its juices, and stir well until heated through. Add tomato sauce and simmer for 5 to 10 minutes, until the sauce has come together and thickened. Reduce heat to low and set aside.

Bring a large pot of salted water to a boil on high heat. Add pasta carefully, a few rags at a time, to prevent sticking. Stir and cook for 3 to 4 minutes, until tender. Drain.

Add pasta to sauce and turn off heat. Stir well, and let the stracci absorb some of the liquid. Divide pasta among 4 bowls and garnish with fresh fennel fronds and salt. Serve immediately.

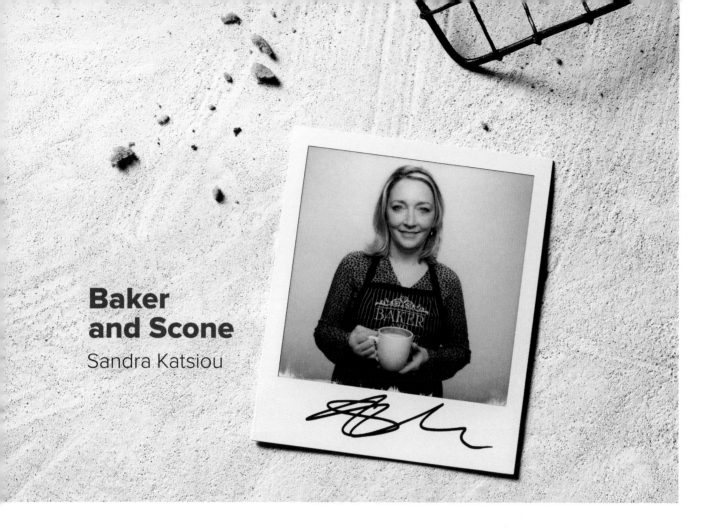

Baker
and Scone

Sandra Katsiou

TORONTO HAS EXPERIENCED an upsurge in restaurants focusing on doing one thing really well, and such is the case with Sandra Katsiou's bake-shop on St. Clair West. In 2014, Katsiou turned a former hair salon into a pretty-as-a-peach bakery café, and following months of anticipation—and perhaps underestimating the power of the scone— promptly sold out. She had no choice but to ramp up production by hiring many more hands. Each small batch of these fluffy, crusty beauties is hand-made, created with a pile of grated butter, pure ingredients, and super flavour kicks such as salted caramel; carrot cake and orange; lemon poppy seed; maple walnut; and cheddar, chive, and dill (there's a rotating roster of more than 50 kinds).

Katsiou was a personal chef before becoming the city's undisputed scone queen, so the shop also does a brisk business in fresh salads, cookies, and warming soups, like the pear and parsnip purée. "I've been making this recipe at my catering events for years," says Katsiou. "It can be served casu-ally, hot out of a mug, or made more elegant for a dinner party with pear crisps." And just as Katsiou learned with her coveted scones, be sure to make extra—there's never enough.

¼ cup olive oil

1 large onion, finely chopped

4 cloves garlic, minced

2 ribs celery, thinly sliced

1 Tbsp garlic powder

1 Tbsp dried tarragon

1 bay leaf

1 tsp freshly ground black pepper

1 tsp kosher salt

4–6 parsnips, peeled and diced

4 Bartlett pears, peeled and diced

4 cups chicken or vegetable stock

1 Tbsp grated lemon zest

Juice of 1 lemon

 Serves 8

Pear and Parsnip Soup

Heat olive oil in a heavy-bottomed saucepan on medium-high. Add onions and cook for 3 to 5 minutes, or until slightly golden. Add garlic, celery, garlic powder, tarragon, bay leaf, pepper, and salt and sauté for another 3 minutes. Add parsnips, pears, and stock and bring to a boil on high heat. Reduce heat to medium and simmer, covered, for 20 minutes. Allow to cool slightly, then transfer to a blender, in batches if necessary, and purée to your desired texture. Season with lemon zest, lemon juice, and additional salt, if needed.

½ cup organic unsalted butter, softened
½ cup granulated sugar
¾ cup brown sugar
1 egg
2 tsp vanilla extract
1 vanilla bean, halved lengthwise
½ cup whole-wheat flour
½ cup all-purpose flour
½ tsp baking soda
1½ cups large flake oats

 **Makes 36 cookies**

Oatmeal Vanilla Bean Cookies

Preheat the oven to 375°F.

In the bowl of a stand mixer fitted with a paddle attachment, combine butter and sugars and mix on medium speed until smooth. Add egg and vanilla extract, scrape in seeds of the vanilla bean, and mix until smooth.

In a separate bowl, mix flours and baking soda together until combined. Add flour mixture to wet mixture and mix for 30 seconds. Add oats and mix until just combined. (Do not overmix.)

Place 2-Tbsp mounds of dough, 2 inches apart, on a baking sheet. Leave dough in a mound, rather than flattening. (This will create thick, chewy cookies.) Bake for 11 to 12 minutes, until golden.

Bar Reyna
Nicki Laborie
and Omar Ma

WHEN SUNSHINE TURNS to snow but there's still a song in your heart, check out Toronto's new hub for al fresco snacks in Yorkville. When Carens Wine and Cheese Bar decamped the pretty Victorian row house with its hidden-gem patio, Bar Reyna filled the void. Owner Nicki Laborie—who spent years running restaurants from New York to St. Martin to Montreal—finally has a place to call her own. Helming the kitchen is Omar Ma, the talented young chef Laborie brought on to create the savoury Greek, Spanish, and Turkish bites. "I like the idea of snack-driven food," says Ma, who has worked at Cava, Buca Yorkville, and 416 Snack Bar. Plates run from *merguez pide* (a Turkish pizza) to spiced pumpkin labneh with pops of pink peppercorns. Lamb baklava, made with braised shank, is a brilliant savoury reinterpretation of a favourite sweet. The space, by Solid Design & Build, is broken up into three unique areas. The Royal Quarters, located downstairs around the bar, is all gold-burnished walls, mirrors, and low lighting. Upstairs, the Moroccan Den is adorned with hanging lanterns, which cast shadows and light around the buzzy room. And then there's the whitewashed Mediterranean Secret Garden, a 48-seat enclosed patio with a retractable roof—one of the city's few winterized spots for alfresco January tipples.

FACING: Spiced Pumpkin Labneh, with Lamb Shank Baklava

Lamb shank

½ cup raisins

1½ cups unsweetened apple juice

Salt and freshly ground black pepper

4 lamb shanks (9 oz each)

6 Tbsp olive oil, divided

3 red onions, finely chopped

8 cloves garlic, finely chopped

2–3 red chilies

1 tsp smoked paprika

3 fresh bay leaves

4 sprigs fresh rosemary

3 Tbsp red wine vinegar

2 cups red wine

1 can (14½ oz) plum tomatoes

3 cups chicken stock

⅓ cup Dijon mustard

½ bunch fresh mint, chopped

1 pack *kataifi* (see Tip)

Kataifi is a Greek pastry shredded into thin strands; the dough is squeezed through a perforated disc onto a hot metal plate, on which it is dried in long strands. It can be purchased at Middle Eastern stores, as well as in the frozen-food sections of some supermarkets.

 Serves 4–6 (about 16–20 pieces)

Lamb Shank Baklava

Lamb shank Preheat the oven to 400°F.

In a small bowl, combine raisins and apple juice and set aside. Generously rub salt and pepper over the lamb shanks until well seasoned. Place shanks in a roasting pan, and roast for 20 minutes.

Meanwhile, heat 4 Tbsp olive oil in a medium braising pot or casserole on medium. Add onions and garlic and sauté for 3 minutes. Add chilies, paprika, bay leaves, and rosemary and cook for another 10 minutes, until onions have softened. Add vinegar and wine and cook for another 5 minutes, or until reduced by half. Add raisins and apple juice and cook for another 12 minutes, until reduced by half. Transfer mixture to a blender and purée until smooth. Return mixture to the pot.

Remove shanks from the oven and reduce temperature to 275°F. Place shanks in the braising pot, add tomatoes and chicken stock, and bring to a boil on high heat. Cover, place in the oven, and braise for 2½ to 3 hours, or until the meat falls off the bone and the sauce has thickened.

In a small bowl, combine mustard and mint and stir to mix. Transfer shanks to a cutting board and set aside to cool. Pull meat apart, season with salt and pepper, and add mustard mixture.

Place 2 feet of plastic wrap on a flat surface. Place a quarter of the lamb along one edge, and wrap the plastic wrap over the mixture, moulding and shaping it into a cylinder. Tie the edges and freeze for 6 to 7 hours to harden.

Meanwhile, defrost kataifi.

Burnt honey and saffron aioli

Makes 2 cups

2 cups mayonnaise

1 clove garlic, grated

Zest and juice of 1 lemon

Salt

2 Tbsp honey

½ tsp saffron

Assembly

¼ cup pistachios, shelled
  and crushed

Burnt honey saffron aioli In a small bowl, combine mayonnaise, garlic, lemon zest and juice, and salt and mix well. Set aside.

Pour honey into a heavy-bottomed pot and bring to a boil on medium-high heat. Cook for 3 minutes, until it begins to caramelize and turns a pale amber. Remove the pot from the heat, stir in saffron, and set aside to cool. Whisk into mayonnaise and set aside.

To assemble Place lamb on a cutting board, remove the plastic, and cut into 1-inch cylinders. Place on a baking sheet. Pull kataifi apart into 6-inch strands and lightly brush with olive oil. Wrap each lamb cylinder with kataifi until it's about 2 inches in diameter. Place baking sheet in fridge for 30 minutes.

Place pistachios in a small pot and toast on medium heat for 6 minutes. Chop and set aside.

Preheat the oven to 350°F.

Heat the remaining 2 Tbsp of oil in a frying pan on medium-high. Sear lamb kataifi for 30 seconds on each side, until lightly golden all around. Using tongs, transfer them to a baking sheet and bake for 6 to 8 minutes, until golden brown. Dollop aioli on 4 to 6 small plates, add 3 to 4 pieces of lamb kataifi to each, and garnish with chopped pistachios. Serve.

Spiced pumpkin purée

1 pumpkin (2¼ lbs), peeled, seeded, and cut into ½-inch cubes (or 2 1-lb cans of store-bought pumpkin)

1½ tsp smoked paprika

1½ tsp ground cinnamon

½ tsp ground allspice

⅓ tsp nutmeg

⅓ tsp cayenne

1 Tbsp honey

Salt

Labneh

4 cups plain Greek yogurt

½ tsp salt

2 cloves garlic, grated

¼ cup fresh lemon juice

3 Tbsp honey

¼ cup Spiced Pumpkin Purée (see here)

Assembly

1 Tbsp unsalted butter

4 fresh sage leaves

1½ tsp pumpkin seeds

1½ tsp sunflower seeds

1 tsp pink peppercorns

4–6 pita breads, sliced

 You may have extra spiced pumpkin purée. It can be preserved for up to seven days in the fridge and can be used in everything from your favourite pasta (it's great in ravioli) to spreading it on toast and topping with a poached egg. Leftover labneh can also be covered and stored in the fridge for several days.

 Serves 4–6

Spiced Pumpkin Labneh

Spiced pumpkin purée If using a fresh pumpkin, bring a large pot of salted water to a boil on high heat. Add pumpkin and cook for 30 minutes, until very tender. Strain water into a bowl and return pumpkin to the pot. Set aside water for later use.

Using a hand blender, purée pumpkin until smooth. Heat in a saucepan on low. Slowly add pumpkin water and stir, until pumpkin has a smooth purée consistency. (It shouldn't be overly runny or dry.)

Transfer purée to a large bowl (or add canned pumpkin to a bowl), add spices and honey, and mix well. Season with salt to taste and refrigerate for 1 to 2 hours, or until cool. (This recipe may make more than you will need for your labneh. See Tip, above, for storing instructions.)

Labneh Line a deep bowl with cheesecloth. In another bowl, combine yogurt and salt and stir well to mix. Pour yogurt into the cloth, bring the cloth edges together, and tie securely with a string. Hang the bundle on the kitchen tap and leave for 24 to 36 hours, until yogurt is thick and dry (it's okay if the centre is creamy). Remove yogurt from the cheesecloth and place into a clean bowl.

Add garlic, lemon juice, honey, and pumpkin purée and, using a spatula, fold mixture until well mixed. Season with salt and place in the fridge for 1 hour, until cooled.

To assemble In a small frying pan on medium-high heat, cook butter for 3 to 4 minutes, until it starts to brown. Add sage and cook for another 30 seconds, until sage is crispy. Stir in seeds and peppercorns.

Spread spiced pumpkin purée into a shallow bowl. Top with labneh in the centre, then spread with the back of a soup spoon. Finish with brown butter mixture. Serve with pita.

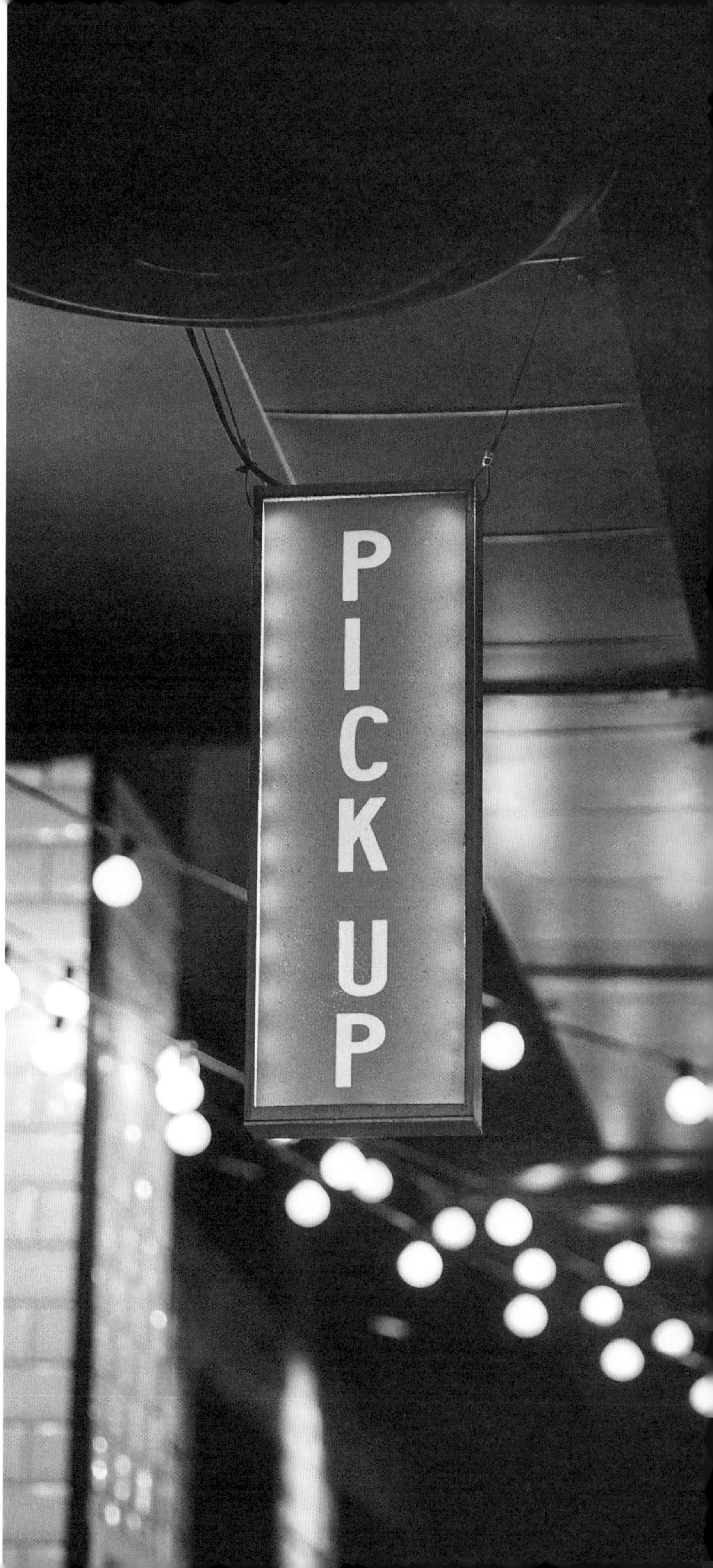
PICK UP

Beaumont Kitchen

Paul Senecal

WHEN I FIRST WALKED into Beaumont Kitchen at Saks Fifth Avenue in Sherway Gardens, I immediately considered changing my life goals and becoming a lady who lunches. The room is comfortably elegant—with soothing neutrals, chevron flooring, and brass light fixtures—and the menu caters to its discerning clientele with share-friendly apps such as beet and feta dip with warm flatbread, and crispy polenta fries with lemon aioli. Salads run from dainty to hearty to a combination of both, as found in the pretty-as-a-picture thai root vegetable salad, a spiralized rainbow of flavours and textures including daikon, beets, carrot, mint, Thai basil, cashews, and a lip-smacking chili-lime dressing. (Tip: ordering this salad means you may have room for a hot fudge sundae for dessert.) Chef de cuisine Paul Senecal acknowledges Torontonians' love for thin-crust pizzas, and so offers several options, including one burbling with four decadent Ontario cheeses. And heartier mains such as flat iron steak and B.C. sockeye salmon with a warm quinoa salad are just the type of Canadian-forward cuisine we've come to know and love from the groundbreaking Oliver & Bonacini restaurant group.

Kosher salt

6 egg yolks (see Tip)

1½ lbs asparagus, ends trimmed

1 jalapeño pepper, thinly sliced into rounds

6 ramp bulbs or 1 bunch green onions, whites only and thinly sliced diagonally

Juice of 3 lemons

4½ Tbsp olive oil

1 tsp salt

3 Tbsp Pusateri's barrel-aged maple syrup

1 Tbsp crispy shallots (see Tip)

 You will probably only need 3 yolks, but once cured, yolks last up to 6 months in an airtight container in the fridge.

Crispy shallots can be found at most Asian grocery stores.

 Serves 6

Asparagus Salad with Cured Egg Yolks

Cover the bottom of a small non-reactive plastic or glass container with a thick layer of salt. Lay egg yolks on salt and *gently* cover with additional salt until yolks can no longer be seen. Cover and let sit in the fridge, untouched, for 2 weeks.

Preheat the oven to 150°F. Line a baking sheet with parchment paper. Gently remove cured eggs from salt and quickly rinse under ice-cold water. Lay yolks on the prepared baking sheet and dry in the oven for 2 hours. Set aside until ready to serve.

Using a vegetable peeler, shave asparagus thinly. (There should be very little waste.) In a mixing bowl, combine asparagus, jalapeño, ramps or green onions, lemon juice, olive oil, and salt and toss. Taste and adjust seasoning if necessary. Divide mixture between 6 bowls, drizzle with maple syrup, and top with a sprinkle of crispy shallots. Gently grate egg yolk over each salad. Enjoy.

Cashew butter

1 cup raw cashews

2 Tbsp tahini

1 cup water

Salt

Chili-lime dressing

3 Anaheim chilies, stemmed

Zest and juice of 6 limes

¼ bunch cilantro stems, washed

⅔ cup white wine vinegar

3 Tbsp honey

2½ tsp salt

1¼ cups vegetable oil

Salad

¾ lb daikon, peeled and trimmed

¾ lb golden beets, peeled and trimmed

¾ lb carrots, peeled and trimmed

¾ lb zucchini, peeled and trimmed

2 tsp salt

½ bunch mint, leaves only

½ bunch Thai basil, leaves only

¾ cup Cashew Butter (see here)

¾ cup Chili-Lime Dressing (see here)

½ bunch cilantro, leaves only

¾ cup cashews, toasted and crushed

 Serves 6

Thai Root Vegetable Salad

Cashew butter Preheat the oven to 350°F. Place cashews on a baking sheet and toast for 12 minutes, or until golden brown. Let cashews cool to room temperature.

Place cashews and tahini in a blender and purée. Gradually add water and purée until smooth and velvety. (You may not need all the water.) Taste and season with salt, if necessary.

Chili-lime dressing Preheat the oven to 400°F. Roast chilies for 3 to 4 minutes, until blistered and slightly charred. Remove from the oven and place in a blender. Add lime zest and juice, cilantro stems, vinegar, honey, and salt and purée until smooth. Gradually add vegetable oil and blend until emulsified. Taste and adjust seasoning, if necessary.

Salad Using a spiralizer, cut daikon into "noodles." Repeat with beets, carrots, and zucchini. Cut spiralled vegetables into 4-inch lengths, place in a large bowl, and add salt. Toss.

Roughly tear mint and basil leaves into 1-inch pieces. Set aside.

Set out 6 salad bowls. Smear 2 Tbsp cashew butter onto the outer edge of each. Divide vegetable mixture equally between the bowls. Pour 2 Tbsp of chili-lime dressing over each salad. Divide herbs equally between the bowls, including cilantro leaves, and top with 2 Tbsp of crushed cashews. Enjoy.

Bestellen

Rob Rossi

ROB ROSSI LOVES MEAT that's naturally raised, locally sourced, and butchered in-house—and he's not afraid to show it. At Bestellen, 40-day dry-aged côte de boeuf is on proud display in the glassed-in meat locker, and it's also illustrated in a beautiful, beastly mural in the main dining room. Naturally, meat is on the menu: oxtail croquettes, the famous Bestellen burger, and a whole suckling pig with all the fixings, served family style. The menu is not light, but it's thoughtful enough to include some vegetarian options, such as celeriac and ricotta agnolotti with roasted honey mushrooms and fried Brussels sprouts that are no afterthought. But for me, it usually comes down to the tartare. "Beef tartare is a staple at the restaurant and is always on our menu in one form or another," says Rossi. For this book, he's written a simple recipe that has a unique twist on a classic, adding olives to complement the beef. "High-quality Greek olives packed in oil will make all the difference," he says. It comes as no surprise that the key to making this dish successful, he notes, is to start by visiting a great butcher.

Pasta
6 eggs
1 teaspoon salt
6 cups "00" flour,
  plus extra for dusting

Pig tail ragu
2 lbs fresh pig tails,
  cleaned by your butcher
¼ cup olive oil, divided
1 teaspoon salt
Freshly ground black pepper
3 ribs celery, cut into 1-inch pieces
1 large onion, cut into 1-inch pieces
1 large carrot, cut into 1-inch pieces

2 cloves garlic, crushed
1 can (5½ oz) tomato paste
1 cup white wine, such as
  Trebbiano
2 bay leaves
1 can (28 fl oz) San Marzano
  tomatoes, crushed by hand
1 bunch basil
¼ cup grated Pecorino Romano

 Serves 4–6

Tagliatelle with Pig Tail Ragu, Basil, and Pecorino

Pasta Crack eggs into a small bowl. Add salt and mix.

In the bowl of a stand mixer fitted with a dough hook, mix flour on medium. Gradually add eggs until dough comes together. (If it's too dry, add a little water. If it's too wet, add a little more flour.) Knead for 5 minutes. Turn dough out onto a board, cover with plastic wrap, and leave to rest for a minimum of 1 hour, or overnight.

Roll out dough through a pasta roller, reducing the thickness one setting at a time (this avoids stressing the dough) until it's nearly paper-thin. Using a sharp knife, cut ribbons of pasta and lay out on a clean surface. Generously sprinkle flour over pasta and set aside to dry, at room temperature, until needed.

Pig tail ragu Preheat the oven to 400°F. Place pig tails on a roasting tray or in a Dutch oven, drizzle with 2 Tbsp olive oil, and add salt and a few grinds of pepper. Toss with your hands and roast for 25 minutes, until golden brown.

Place celery, onions, carrots, and garlic in a food processor and process until finely cut. Set aside.

Remove pig tails from the oven and reduce temperature to 300°F. Using a slotted spoon, transfer pig tails to a plate. Pour off half the fat from the roasting tray or Dutch oven. Place the roasting tray back on the stovetop, add vegetables to the pan, and cook on medium heat for 5 minutes, until vegetables are golden. Add tomato paste and cook for another 5 minutes. Add wine and bay leaves and cook for 2 minutes. Add canned tomatoes and bring sauce to a simmer. Add roasted pig tails back to the pan. (If the tails are not completely covered in sauce, add a small amount of water.) Cover and cook in the oven for 2 hours, or until the meat falls off the bone.

To finish sauce, skim off any excess fat from the surface and transfer pig tails to a cutting board. Remove meat from the bones. Place 3 cups of sauce in a large saucepan and add the meat. (Any remaining sauce can be refrigerated for several days.) Tear basil, add to the saucepan, and season with salt and pepper to taste. Simmer on medium heat while pasta is cooking.

Bring a large pot of salted water to a boil on high heat, add pasta, and cook for 2 minutes until pasta floats, then cook 1 minute longer. Drain, add pasta to sauce, and cook for another 2 minutes. Divide pasta between serving bowls, drizzle with the remaining 2 Tbsp of olive oil, and sprinkle with Pecorino Romano.

1 lb beef tenderloin or strip loin

2 small shallots, finely minced

¼ cup black olives packed in oil, drained, pitted, and finely chopped

½ bunch chives, finely chopped

¼ bunch flat-leaf parsley, finely chopped

1 tsp Dijon mustard, plus extra to serve

Salt and freshly ground black pepper

Juice of ½ a lemon

¼ cup extra-virgin olive oil, plus extra to drizzle and to serve

Sliced onions, to garnish (optional)

Toasted baguette, sliced, to serve (optional)

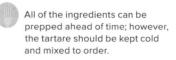 All of the ingredients can be prepped ahead of time; however, the tartare should be kept cold and mixed to order.

 Serves 4–6

Beef Tartare with Black Olives, Lemon, and Olive Oil

Fill a medium bowl with ice. Using a sharp knife, cut beef into a very small dice and transfer to a slightly smaller bowl set over the ice. (The key to this dish is keeping the meat cold.) Add shallots and olives and mix well. Add chives, parsley, Dijon, and salt and pepper to taste. Combine, then add lemon juice and olive oil. Taste and adjust seasoning, if necessary.

Set out serving plates. Lightly pack tartare into a ring mould and turn out onto the plates. Drizzle with olive oil and garnish with sliced onion, if using. Serve as is or with toasted baguette, if using, Dijon and olive oil.

Blackbird Baking Co.

Simon Blackwell

WITH ITS WINDOWS full of everything you want to eat—pointy baguettes, buttery croissants, daily sandwiches, and signature sourdough loaves— this small neighbourhood bakery has grown to become a wholesaler of sourdough breads to retailers across the city. The Kensington Market space is all exposed brick and weathered wood, and Simon Blackwell is the thoughtful chef-turned- artisan baker behind the product. "I had tasted some amazing sourdough breads when travelling in cities like London, New York, and Montreal," he says. "I wanted to bring that to Toronto, where at the time it was very hard to come by." He's talking about 100 percent naturally leavened, hand-shaped breads with an emphasis on wholegrain flours sourced from local mills. A recipe for success, right? Well, at first, people didn't understand what he was doing. "They would come in and ask 'Why is the bread so dark?' or 'Why is it burnt?'" he recollects. "But I was trying to do something different, pushing the colour so that the bread was nice and dark with a hard crust and extra flavour." Blackwell took customers' questions as an opportunity to educate them, slicing into loaves so that the curious could taste that it wasn't burnt, but was in fact the perfect expression of sourdough bread—found in this perfect expres- sion of a bakery.

⅜ cup cold water

1¼ tsp molasses

1⅓ tsp olive oil

¼ cup pumpkin seeds, toasted

½ cup + 1 Tbsp all-purpose flour,
plus extra for dusting

¾ cup + 1 Tbsp rye flour

½ Tbsp brown sugar

1 tsp salt

1 tsp nigella seeds

¼ tsp anise seeds

 **Makes about a dozen crackers**

Rye Crackers

Preheat the oven to 350°F. Line a baking sheet with parchment paper.

In a small bowl, combine water, molasses, and olive oil and mix well. Set aside.

Place pumpkin seeds in a food processor and pulse until finely ground. Transfer to the bowl of a stand mixer fitted with a paddle attachment, add flours, brown sugar, salt, and nigella and anise seeds. Mix on low, gradually adding the wet ingredients, then mix for another 1 minute, until dough comes together.

Turn dough onto a lightly floured surface and roll out as thin as possible. Cut into 2 x 6-inch strips, place on the prepared baking sheet, and bake for 15 to 17 minutes, until golden brown. Store in an airtight container for up to 2 weeks.

2½ cups all-purpose flour, plus
    extra for dusting

1 tsp salt

1 tsp granulated sugar

½ tsp instant yeast

¾ cup grated Pecorino Romano

1½ cups water

Olive oil, for greasing

Coarse sea salt

4 Tbsp chopped mixed herbs
    (e.g., rosemary, parsley, and
    oregano)

 **Makes 1 (10-inch) focaccia**

Pecorino Focaccia Bianca

In a large bowl, combine flour, salt, sugar, yeast, and Pecorino Romano. Stir well. Add water and mix by hand until combined, then mix for another minute. (The dough will be very wet and sticky.) Lightly oil a large bowl, place dough in it, and cover. Set aside for 9 to 12 hours, until dough has more than doubled in size and is covered with bubbles.

Generously dust a clean work surface with flour and use a bowl scraper (or rubber spatula) to scrape dough out of the bowl in one piece. Using floured hands, gently fold dough from the edges to the centre to make a loose ball. Brush with olive oil and sprinkle sea salt over the surface. Cover and set aside for 1 to 2 hours, until almost doubled in size.

Preheat the oven to 450°F and place a rack in the middle slot. Place a pizza stone on the rack to warm.

Meanwhile, generously dust a pizza peel or baking sheet with flour and place dough in the middle. Working quickly to prevent dough from sticking to the peel, use your fingers to dimple the dough in an outward motion, making it an even thickness across the peel. Continue until it reaches a 10-inch diameter. Drizzle with olive oil, top with chopped herbs, and sprinkle generously with additional sea salt.

Shake dough onto the baking stone and bake for 20 minutes, or until crust is a deep golden colour. Transfer focaccia to a cooling rack and let sit for a few minutes before cutting.

Boralia
Wayne Morris

A PINE NEEDLE–FUELLED smoking gun is set under a glass cloche filled with buttery mussels just before the dish is served. The result is a dreamscape of ocean, forest, and deliciousness. The first documented case of man turning needles into cuisine came from Jacques Cartier, who wrote in "Voyages to Canada" (c. 1534) about a tea made with pine needles and bark that saved his ice-stranded crew. These days, chefs Wayne Morris and Evelyn Wu, the husband-and-wife duo behind Boralia, a cozy jewel-box on Ossington, are setting flame to needles and impressing guests with signature dishes like the aforementioned *l'éclade*—a historic dish from France that was introduced to Canada by Samuel de Champlain

in 1605. With a combined history that saw Wu researching alongside Heston Blumenthal and Morris celebrating his Acadian heritage out west, the duo delves into recipes from First Nations peoples, early settlers, and later immigrants, such as the first waves of Chinese to Canada. Some dishes, like devilled Chinese tea eggs and the irresistible pigeon pie, are even time-stamped on the menu (c. 1860 and c. 1611, respectively). But history is made anew with recipes such as baked Eel Lake oysters with shrimp hollandaise (a perfect mouthful), cured trout grilled over cedar branches, and wood nettle spätzle with confit egg yolk. This is Canada in 2017.

Confit egg yolks	Wood nettle spätzle	Asparagus
6 egg yolks	4 eggs	2 lbs local asparagus, woody
Olive oil	¼ cup whole milk	ends trimmed and reserved
	1½ tsp salt	**Assembly**
	2 cups wood nettle leaves	2 Tbsp unsalted butter
	¼ tsp nutmeg, freshly grated	Salt
	1½ cups all-purpose flour, sifted	Freshly ground black pepper
		Baby arugula

 Serves 6

Wood Nettle Spätzle with Asparagus and Confit Egg Yolk

Confit egg yolks Preheat the oven to 150°F. Place eggs yolks in a small ovenproof pot and gently cover with olive oil. Place in oven and cook for 50 minutes, until the outer layer of the yolks has begun to set but still quiver. They should be the consistency of the interior of a soft-boiled egg. Set aside.

Wood nettle spätzle Place eggs, milk, salt, nettle leaves, and nutmeg in a blender and blend until smooth. Transfer mixture to a large bowl, add flour, and whisk for 2 minutes, or until smooth and slightly elastic. Let stand 30 minutes.

Bring a pot of water to boil. Set a spätzle maker or a large-holed colander about 3 inches from the surface of the water. Place half of the batter in the spätzle maker or colander, and, using a spatula, press batter through the holes so that it falls into the water in tear drop–shaped pieces. Cook spätzle for 2 minutes, or until they float on the surface. Using a slotted spoon, immediately transfer spätzle to a bowl of ice water. Repeat the process with remaining batter. Remove spätzle from water.

Asparagus Preheat a grill or oven to 400°F. Cut the lower portion of the asparagus into coins until the upper portion is about 3 to 4 inches long. Set coins aside. Grill or roast asparagus spears for 2 minutes, or until just cooked. Transfer grilled asparagus to a plate.

To assemble In a heavy-bottomed, non-stick frying pan on medium-high heat, melt butter. Add spätzle and asparagus coins and sauté, stirring constantly, for 2 to 3 minutes, until golden brown. Season with salt and pepper to taste.

Divide spätzle onto 6 plates. Make a well in the centre of each plate and, using a perforated spoon, gently remove each egg yolk from oil and place in the well. Season each yolk with salt to taste. Place grilled asparagus spears on top of spätzle and top with baby arugula. Serve immediately.

Trout

3 Tbsp sea salt
2 Tbsp granulated sugar
1 Tbsp brown sugar
¼ tsp ground white pepper
¼ tsp ground allspice
¼ tsp broken bay leaf
2 boneless, skinless trout fillets
  (5 oz each)

Gin sour cream

2 Tbsp sour cream
½ Tbsp gin (e.g., Ungava or
  Dillon's Rose Gin)

Pickled ramps

¼ lb well-formed mature ramps
¼ cup rice vinegar
¼ cup water
⅛ cup sugar

Charred onions

4–5 golf ball–sized cipollini or
  pearl onions
1–1½ cups buttermilk
Salt
1 Tbsp neutral oil (e.g., grapeseed)

 Boralia uses only ethically foraged ramps. Forbes Wild Foods is a great Toronto source.

Assembly

Cedar branches
Wild greens (e.g., chickweed
  or sorrel)
A few drops of birch syrup
Piment d'espelette, or any fine
  ground chili powder

 Serves 4

Cured Trout Grilled over Cedar with Gin Sour Cream, Pickled Ramps, and Charred Onion

Trout In a bowl, combine salt, sugars, pepper, allspice, and bay leaf and mix well. Rub the cure on trout fillets and place fish in a resealable plastic bag. Refrigerate for 3 hours, turning once every hour. Rinse trout under cold running water and pat dry with paper towel. Thinly slice on the bias.

Gin sour cream Combine ingredients in a small bowl and set aside in fridge.

Pickled ramps Cut ramp greens from bulbs and reserve for later use. (They can be sautéed or made into pesto.)

In a small pot, combine vinegar, water, and sugar and bring to a boil on high heat. Add ramp bulbs, reduce heat to medium-low, and simmer gently for 5 minutes. Cool.

Charred onions In a medium saucepan on low heat, combine onions, enough buttermilk to cover, and salt and poach for 20 minutes, until tender. Cool and drain, reserving buttermilk for another use.

Slice onions in half. In a heavy-bottomed pan on high, heat oil, add onions, cut-side down, and char for 2 minutes, or until desired colour is reached. Set aside to cool, and then separate onions into small rings.

To assemble Preheat a grill. Roll up trout slices and place on a wire rack. Place a few cedar branches on the grill. When branches start to exude smoke, place wire rack with trout on top of branches, cover, and gently smoke for about 1 minute.

Transfer trout to a plate and arrange with the pickled ramps, charred onions, and dots of the sour cream mixture. Garnish with wild greens, and add birch syrup and chili powder. Serve as is or on bagels or with potatoes.

Byblos

Stuart Cameron

EXECUTIVE CHEF STUART Cameron's intoxicating Middle Eastern shared plates are simply irresistible, taking inspiration from some of the Mediterranean and Levant's greatest culinary countries. To match the food, restaurateurs Hanif Harji and Charles Khabouth created the glossy two-storey space in the theatre district as a sophisticated mecca for mezzes and good times. Slide into a banquette, forget your troubles, and let the good times ride with a date old-fashioned or glasses of magically milky arak. Then say yes to a dozen of Cameron's triumphant takes, such as house-made labneh, crispy eggplant with house

yogurt, duck kibbeh, slow-roasted Ontario lamb, and Mejadra rice topped with lentils, fried shallots, and labneh. Not just for vegetarian Moosewood types, the herbaceous and creamy green goddess dressing finds its way atop a hot, cool, and crispy falafel salad—and into this cookbook. With all of the senses now in high gear, the pavlova arrives as a dreamy wash of rose pastry cream, pomegranate molasses, and *pashmak*, a Persian cotton candy. It is perhaps Cameron's most beautiful take on these seductive flavours from faraway lands.

Pickled red onion
1 red onion, halved lengthwise and sliced
½ cup boiling water
¼ cup red wine vinegar
3 Tbsp granulated sugar
1¼ tsp kosher salt

Sabzi's green goddess dressing
⅓ cup flat-leaf parsley leaves
⅓ cup cilantro leaves
2 Tbsp chopped fresh chervil
2 Tbsp chopped fresh dill
2 Tbsp chopped green onions, green part only
1 Tbsp dried fenugreek leaves
1 clove garlic
⅓ cup sour cream
⅓ cup mayonnaise
Juice of ½ a lemon
Kosher salt

Falafel
¾ cup dried chickpeas
¼ tsp baking soda
1 cup chopped flat-leaf parsley
1 cup chopped cilantro
½ tsp smoked paprika
½ tsp ground cumin
2 shallots, finely chopped
3 cloves garlic, crushed
¼ tsp cayenne
Kosher salt
All-purpose flour (optional)
4 cups vegetable oil, for deep-frying

Puffed amaranth
¼ cup raw amaranth

Assembly
6 heads baby gem lettuce
½ quantity Pickled Red Onion (see here)
3 radishes, thinly sliced
2 oz Macedonian feta, broken up
1 package (2 oz) pea tendrils, for garnish
3 Tbsp extra-virgin olive oil
4 Tbsp Puffed Amaranth (see here)
Sea salt

 Serves 4 (as an appetizer)

Falafel Salad

Pickled red onion Place all ingredients into a bowl, mix well, and set aside for 24 hours.

Sabzi's green goddess dressing Place herbs, green onions, fenugreek, garlic, and sour cream into a blender and process for 1 minute, or until smooth. Add mayonnaise and blend until just combined. Season with lemon juice and salt. Set aside.

Falafel Place chickpeas and baking soda in a large bowl, add 8 cups of water, and soak overnight. Drain, then rinse well. Pat dry with paper towels.

Place chickpeas, parsley, cilantro, paprika, cumin, shallots, garlic, and cayenne into the bowl of a food processor and process until mixture resembles wet breadcrumbs. Season to taste with salt.

Scoop 1½ Tbsp of mixture and, using your hands, roll tightly into a ball. (If mix feels too wet, add a little flour; if it's too dry, add water to moisten, just enough so that it holds together.) Repeat with remaining mixture. Set aside until ready to fry.

Heat oil in a deep fryer or deep saucepan on medium heat until it reaches a temperature of 340°F. Working in batches, carefully lower falafel into the oil and deep-fry for 4 to 5 minutes, until crispy. Using a slotted spoon, transfer falafel to a plate lined with paper towels. Season with salt.

Puffed amaranth Heat a heavy-bottomed pot on medium-high heat. Add 1 Tbsp amaranth and give the pot a quick shake to evenly spread. Cook for 1 to 2 minutes, uncovered, until amaranth pops. (You'll have the right heat setting once it starts to pop within a few seconds.) Transfer amaranth into a bowl and repeat until all is popped. (Makes 1 cup)

To assemble Separate lettuce leaves and wash, then pat dry with paper towels. Place whole lettuce leaves in a large mixing bowl. Add green goddess dressing and toss well. Arrange leaves in a large salad bowl or on 4 individual plates.

Break falafel in half and arrange pieces on top of lettuce. Top with pickled red onion, radishes, and feta. Garnish with pea tendrils. Drizzle with olive oil and sprinkle with puffed amaranth. Season with salt and serve.

Yogurt sauce

1½ tsp cornstarch

1 egg, beaten

1 shallot, finely chopped

1 cup thick Greek yogurt

⅓ cup dry white wine

2 tsp finely chopped chives

Juice of 1 lemon

Kosher salt

Walnut crumb

¼ cup unsalted butter

3 slices white bread, crusts removed, and diced (about 1½ cups)

⅔ cup toasted walnuts, finely chopped

2 Tbsp finely chopped flat-leaf parsley

2 Tbsp finely chopped fresh dill

Kosher salt, to taste

Brown butter

⅓ cup unsalted butter

Fluke

4 Tbsp extra-virgin olive oil

4 portions skinless and boneless fluke (4 oz each) (ask your fishmonger to do this)

Kosher salt

½ cup Yogurt Sauce

¼ cup Brown Butter (see here)

2 cups Walnut Crumb (see here)

Fresh chervil, for garnish

 Serves 4

Yogurt-Baked Fluke

Yogurt sauce In a bowl, combine cornstarch and egg and whisk together. Add remaining ingredients and mix well. Set aside.

Walnut crumb Preheat the oven to 275°F. In a frying pan on medium heat, melt butter, add diced bread, and stir to coat. Transfer bread to a baking dish and bake for 5 to 10 minutes, until brown and crisp. Transfer croutons to a plate lined with paper towel and drain. Smash croutons into crumbs with the base of a pot.

Place crumbs in a bowl. Add walnuts, parsley, and dill and stir. Season with salt.

Brown butter In a heavy-bottomed medium saucepan on low heat, cook butter for about 10 minutes, or until golden brown and nutty smelling. The butter will foam a bit before it starts to brown, so keep an eye on it. Remove from the heat and set aside to cool for 20 minutes.

Fluke Preheat the broiler. Heat oil in non-stick pan set on medium heat. Season both sides of fish, place it in the pan, and sear for 2 minutes, or until golden and medium-rare. (You are only searing one side.) Transfer to a plate.

Divide yogurt sauce between 4 copper boats (found at your local Indian grocery store) or oven-proof dishes. Place a fluke portion, seared-side up, into each boat, keeping the fish centred. Heat gently on stovetop on medium and simmer for 2 minutes.

Place the boats in the oven and grill for 2 to 3 minutes, until the top of the yogurt sauce has browned slightly. Remove the boats from the oven and spoon 1 Tbsp of brown butter over each fluke. Add ¼ cup of walnut crumb on top and around the fluke and garnish with sprigs of chervil. Serve immediately, with ½ charred lemon if desired.

Carmen Cocina Española

Luis Valenzuela Robles Linares

LAUNCHED DURING TORONTO'S great Spanish reawakening of 2013, when tapas and paella were on everyone's lips, Carmen Cocina Española (co-owned by Veronica Carmen Laudes and chef Luis Valenzuela Robles Linares) was leading the charge with garlicky charcoal-fired shrimp and paellas that taste like the crusty beauties in Valencia. "It all starts with the actual pan," says Valenzuela of his signature vessel. "There is something very special about the paella dish; its roundness is inclusive and brings people to the table." The hospitality is certainly felt both inside the restaurant and on the back patio full of flowers and lights, tapas, and dry sherry. Manchego-stuffed dates are wrapped in bacon and sprinkled

with crushed Marconas. Heirloom tomatoes are served with creamy burrata, grilled Ontario peaches, and tempura squash flowers. Ceviche de trucha is seared trout in a lip-smacking Aji "tiger's milk." Valenzuela stops by to explain the origin of his sticky, smoky dates: "An old man is planting date trees in the desert even though they won't bear fruit until long after he's gone. When a young boy passing by asks why, the old man says it's so that others will enjoy them." This story, which holds special meaning for Valenzuela, has become the foundation of the hospitality you feel while dining at Carmen.

Brine

1 star anise
2 Tbsp juniper berries
1 morita or chipotle chili
12½ cups water
1 cup ground espresso
1 cup salt
½ cup agave syrup
¼ cup granulated sugar
4 duck breasts
   (5–7 oz each), skin on

Mole

6 Roma tomatoes
2 Tbsp + ¼ cup vegetable
   oil, divided
Salt and freshly ground
   black pepper
1 dried chipotle chili, halved
   lengthwise and seeded
2 dried ancho chilies, halved
   lengthwise and seeded
2 dried morita chilies, halved
   lengthwise and seeded
2 cups chicken stock, divided
2 small onions, finely chopped

1 clove garlic, finely chopped
2 cloves
1 tsp ground cinnamon
1 tsp black pepper
2 Tbsp raisins
2 Tbsp ground toasted
   peanuts (optional)
2 Tbsp toasted and ground
   sesame seeds
1 cup tortilla chips
½ cup bittersweet
   chocolate, chopped
Salt
Wine vinegar

Assembly

3 Tbsp vegetable oil
Pomegranate seeds,
   for garnish

 Serves 4

Pato con Mole

Brine In a dry frying pan set on low heat, combine star anise, juniper berries, and chili and toast for 1 to 2 minutes, until fragrant. Transfer spices to a large pot, add water, espresso, salt, syrup, and sugar and bring to boil on high heat. Remove from the heat and allow to cool to room temperature. (The brine can be made the day before and refrigerated.)

Add duck breasts to brine and refrigerate for 24 hours. Remove duck breasts from brine and pat dry with paper towels. Refrigerate for another 6 hours.

Mole Preheat the oven to 350°F. Cut tomatoes in half. Place tomatoes in a bowl, add 2 Tbsp vegetable oil, and season with a pinch of salt and pepper. Place on a baking tray, face-side up, and roast for 10 to 15 minutes, or until soft. Set aside.

Place dried chilies on a baking sheet and toast for 5 minutes, or until fragrant.

To a small saucepan on medium-high heat, add ½ cup chicken stock and heat through. Remove the pan from the heat, add chilies, and soak for 10 minutes, or until softened. Place chilies and stock into a blender and blend until a paste is formed. Set aside.

Heat ¼ cup vegetable oil in a large frying pan on medium-high. Add onions and sauté for 7 minutes, until translucent. Add garlic and cook for another minute, until fragrant. Stir in cloves, cinnamon, and black pepper. Add chili paste, reduce heat to low, and cook for another 10 minutes.

Add roasted tomatoes and the remaining 1½ cups chicken stock and cook for 5 minutes on medium heat. Add raisins, peanuts (if using), sesame seeds, tortilla chips, and chocolate. Reduce heat to low and cook for 45 minutes.

Let mixture cool slightly, then place in a blender and purée until smooth. (If necessary, add a bit more chicken stock to thin out to a sauce-like consistency.) Add salt and wine vinegar to taste. Return mole to a saucepan and keep warm on low heat.

To assemble Preheat the oven to 350°F. Heat vegetable oil in an ovenproof frying pan on medium, add duck breasts, skin-side down, and sear for 5 minutes, until the skin is crisp and golden. Flip over, then transfer the pan to the oven. Cook for 15 minutes, until cooked through. Set aside for 5 minutes to rest.

To serve, slice duck breasts, fan out onto 4 plates, and cover with mole. Garnish with pomegranate seeds and serve immediately.

2 Tbsp Arbequina olive oil

2 bone-in chicken thighs, cut into quarters (ask your butcher to do this)

1 semi-cured chorizo sausage, cut into quarters

6 shrimp (e.g., B.C. spot prawns), heads on

1 small onion, finely minced

¼ red pepper, seeded and finely chopped

¼ yellow or green pepper, seeded and finely chopped

1 clove garlic, minced

½ small zucchini, finely chopped

¼ cup halved snow peas

1 tsp paprika

Salt

Pinch of saffron

1 cup bomba rice

3 cups chicken stock, divided

½ cup snap peas

1 cup mussels, cleaned

1 cup clams, cleaned

6 basil leaves, for garnish

1 lemon, cut into wedges, for garnish (optional)

 Serves 4

Paella del Carmen

Heat olive oil in a large paella pan or frying pan on medium. Add chicken and cook for 20 minutes, until well browned. Transfer to a plate. Add chorizo and cook for 2 minutes. Transfer to a separate plate. Add shrimp and cook for 2 to 3 minutes, until shells are opaque. Transfer to the plate of chorizo and set aside.

In the same pan, add onions and cook on medium-low heat for 10 minutes, or until translucent. Add peppers, stir, and cook for another 10 minutes. Add garlic, zucchini, and snow peas and cook for another 10 minutes. Add paprika, salt, and saffron, and then stir in rice.

Return chicken thighs to the pan, add 1 cup stock (enough to cover), and bring to a boil on medium-high heat. Gradually add remainder of stock, ½ cup at a time, and simmer for 10 minutes. Add snap peas, mussels, and clams, cooking for 5 minutes, or until clam and mussel shells have opened. Leave the pan of rice undisturbed (to release the gluten in the rice, which gives the paella a nice starchy finish). Discard any clams or mussels that have not opened.

Return chorizo and shrimp to the pan and cook for another 5 minutes. You want to build a light crust, known as *socorat*, at the bottom of the pan, which is the prized part of the paella.

Turn off the heat and let the paella rest, covered, for 5 to 8 minutes before eating. Scatter basil leaves over the paella and serve with a lemon wedge, if using.

Carver
Robert Bragagnolo

THIS POCKET-SIZED RESTAURANT, plunked down on Peter Street, is a lofty square slab of polished concrete and glass where downtown worker bees and condo dwellers come for slow-roasted done right. Chef and owner Rob Bragagnolo was born of a lineage of Italian chefs (his grandfather had a trattoria in Veneto from which Carver's signature porchetta recipe borrows) and trained at restaurants in Spain, eventually going on to co-own and operate a Michelin-starred restaurant in Palma de Mallorca. Open shelving showcases cans of Brio and pickled peppers (the quick-service spot was sparingly but skillfully designed by co-owner Sergio Fiorino). Menu items, one per clipboard, are featured on a statement wall and flap in the summer breeze. Their porchetta is brined for

hours, then seasoned with herbs like rosemary and fennel pollen before being roasted for many more. It comes piled onto focaccia custom baked by the Drake Hotel, and topped with house-made roasted red pepper pesto, salsa verde aioli, and a sprinkling of crackling crumble. Transform that sandwich into a hearty plate instead, siding the hormone- and antibiotic-free, Mennonite-raised pork or roast chicken with equally elevated offerings like the avocado kale Caesar salad. Carver started as Toronto's first UberEats pop-up and has since become living proof of the maxim "If you build it, they will eat it."

Chicken
1 lemon, halved
½ bunch fresh thyme
2 Tbsp salt, divided
1 free-run or organic chicken (2 lbs)
1 tsp freshly ground black pepper
1 Tbsp Spanish smoked paprika
1 tsp chili flakes

Tomato pesto
1 clove garlic
2 ripe tomatoes
3 Tbsp sun-dried tomatoes, chopped
½ bunch fresh basil
1 tsp salt
6 Tbsp extra-virgin olive oil

Lemon mayonnaise
1 lemon, whole
¼ cup cold water
1 cup mayonnaise

Assembly
1 rosemary focaccia loaf
Fresh basil leaves

 Serves 4–6

Chicken Sandwich

Chicken Preheat the oven to 425°F.

Place lemon, thyme, and a pinch of salt into the chicken cavity. Season the outside of the chicken by liberally rubbing it with 1 Tbsp salt, pepper, paprika, and chili flakes. Place chicken in a roasting pan and roast for 30 minutes.

Reduce the oven temperature to 250°F and roast for another 25 minutes, or until the juices run clear. Remove chicken from the oven and set aside to rest for 35 minutes.

Tomato pesto In a mortar and pestle, combine garlic, tomatoes, and sun-dried tomatoes. Add basil, salt, and olive oil and continue to mash until a smooth paste is formed. (Alternatively, combine all ingredients in a blender and pulse until smooth.) Season to taste.

Lemon mayonnaise Preheat the oven to 500°F. Roast lemon for 12 minutes, until lightly browned.

Carefully place lemon in a blender, add water, and blend for 4 minutes until smooth. Set aside to cool to room temperature, then fold into mayonnaise.

To assemble Preheat the oven to 450°F.

Carve chicken. Cut focaccia in half and spread tomato pesto on one half. Place chicken slices on top. Spread lemon mayonnaise on the other half of the bread and garnish with fresh basil. Carefully place sides together to form whole sandwich.

Place sandwich on a baking sheet and grill for 90 seconds on each side. Cut into 4 to 6 pieces and serve immediately.

Avocado dressing

2 avocados, peeled and pitted

Juice of 1 lemon

¼ cup avocado oil

¼ cup cold water

2 Tbsp grated Parmigiano-Reggiano

½ clove garlic, finely chopped

¼ anchovy filet, finely chopped

1 Tbsp salt

Salad

6 strips bacon

2 bunches kale, shredded

1 romaine lettuce heart, coarsely chopped

4 Tbsp Avocado Dressing (see here)

Salt

4 Tbsp grated Parmigiano-Reggiano

1 avocado, sliced

1 cup croutons

1 lemon, cut into wedges (optional)

 Serves 4–6

Avocado Kale Caesar Salad

Avocado dressing Place avocado, lemon juice, avocado oil, and water into a blender and blend for 1 to 2 minutes, until smooth and creamy. Add Parmigiano-Reggiano, garlic, anchovy, and salt and purée for another 30 seconds, until well incorporated. (If mixture is too thick, add more cold water.) Refrigerate until needed. Makes approximately 1 cup.

Salad Preheat the oven to 400°F. Place bacon on a baking tray and bake for 7 to 8 minutes, or until crispy.

Place kale and romaine in a large bowl, add dressing, and mix thoroughly to coat. Add a pinch of salt to taste, and add more dressing if desired. Place dressed leaves in a large serving bowl, sprinkle with Parmigiano-Reggiano, and top with avocado, bacon, and croutons. Serve with lemon wedges, if using.

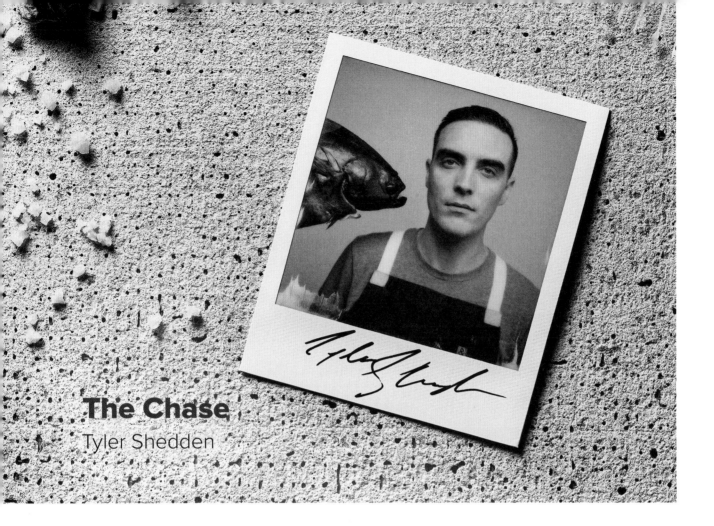

The Chase
Tyler Shedden

THE CHASE HOSPITALITY Group has ushered in a new era of comfortable fine dining in Toronto, and this glowing penthouse space atop a heritage building on Temperance Street—full of chandeliers and swish banquettes—was the torch that lit the fire, after which came Little Fin, Fish and Oyster, Colette, Kasa Moto, and Planta. If you don't see culinary director and chef Tyler Shedden in the kitchen, it's probably because he's off in Vancouver meeting with fishers like Steve Johansen from Organic Ocean, buying up lingcod on the docks at False Creek. And you can taste the thoughtfulness, from line to plate. I often think back fondly to a dining experience I had a year ago, where a halibut for two had been deboned and served tableside by the restaurant's captain. Seafood, from fresh platters to roasted octopus tossed with salsa verde and merguez, is the main draw, while Cornish hen and vegetable mains such as spinach cavatelli with rapini pesto are equally opulent. You'll want to leave room for desserts like the chocolate chip brownie with salted peanut butter caramel. Why rush out when you can relax amidst all of this indulgence?

FACING: Brioche-Crusted Nova Scotia Halibut with Morels and Wild Leek–Brown Butter Tartare Sauce

Pickled wild leeks

1 lb wild leeks

1 cup water

1¼ cups white wine vinegar or apple cider vinegar

4 Tbsp maple syrup

1 Tbsp kosher or other non-iodized salt

½ tsp whole mustard seeds

½ tsp whole coriander seeds

6–8 whole black peppercorns

2 sprigs fresh dill

1 clove garlic, minced

Brioche crust

1 loaf brioche (750 g), diced

⅔ cups unsalted butter, room temperature

6 wild leek greens, finely minced

1 Tbsp finely chopped parsley

1 tsp fresh thyme leaves

 Serves 4

Brioche-Crusted Nova Scotia Halibut with Morels and Wild Leek–Brown Butter Tartare Sauce

Pickled wild leeks To clean leeks, trim off the string roots at the bottom, then wash well. Slice leeks a little bit above the point where the white part ends and the green leaves separate out. Set aside the leaves for later use. (You're only going to pickle the bulbs with a bit of the green attached.)

To make the brine, combine water, vinegar, maple syrup, and salt in a small saucepan. Add mustard seeds, coriander seeds, and peppercorns and bring to a boil on high heat. Reduce heat to low and simmer for 5 minutes.

Add dill and garlic to 1 or 2 canning jars (depending on size). Lay leeks in with the bulb toward the bottom, packing them so tightly that there is no room for any more. (This ensures that the leeks stay immersed in the brine rather than float up out of it.) Leave half an inch of headspace between the top of the leeks and the rim of each jar. Pour hot brine over the leeks. Cover them completely, but leave between a quarter of an inch and half an inch of headspace between the liquid and the top of the jar. Screw on the canning lid.

Fill a saucepan half full with water, bring to a boil on high heat, and add the jars, taking care that the jars are fully submerged in the boiling water. Boil for 10 minutes, then set aside to cool.

Wait at least a week for the flavours to develop before sampling (they will improve after a month). The pickled wild leeks will keep, unopened, at room temperature for at least a year. Once opened, store in the fridge for up to 2 months.

Brioche crust Place brioche in a blender or food processor and pulse until crumb-like in texture.

In the bowl of stand mixer fitted with the paddle attachment, combine 1½ cups of brioche crumbs and remaining ingredients. Mix for 2 minutes on medium until well incorporated.

Line a baking sheet with parchment paper and spread mixture in an even thickness across the whole tray. Cover with another sheet of parchment and use a rolling pin to roll mixture out until it reaches an even thickness of one-eighth of an inch. Refrigerate or freeze until firm.

Once firm, cut into rectangles or shapes the size of your halibut fillets and set aside in the fridge.

Tartare sauce

¾ cup + 2 Tbsp unsalted butter
¼ cup baby capers, rinsed
Zest and juice of 2 lemons
6 bulbs Pickled Wild Leeks,
   thinly sliced (see here)
1 shallot, finely chopped
1 Tbsp finely chopped parsley
Salt

Mushroom broth

2 Tbsp olive oil
2 Tbsp unsalted butter
3 Tbsp minced shallots
½ lb morel mushrooms, cleaned
1 lb hen-of-the-woods mushrooms,
   cleaned
1 lb baby spinach, cleaned
   and stemmed
½ cup white wine
¼ cup crème fraîche
Juice of 1 lemon
1 Tbsp chopped fresh tarragon
1 Tbsp cold butter
1 Tbsp truffle oil
3 Tbsp chopped chives
Salt and freshly ground black pepper

Halibut

1 Tbsp olive oil
4 halibut fillets (8 oz each), preferably
   sustainably sourced
Sea salt
¼ cup unsalted butter, cold

Tartare sauce In a medium saucepan set on medium heat, melt butter. Cook, whisking occasionally, until the milk solids have turned golden brown and smell nutty (be careful not to let the solids burn).

Stir remaining ingredients into the warm brown butter until well incorporated. Adjust seasoning with salt and set aside.

Mushroom broth Heat olive oil and butter in a large sauté pan on medium-high. Add shallots and sauté for 5 minutes, until tender. Add mushrooms and slowly roast on the stovetop for 5 to 7 minutes, until lightly browned. Add spinach and white wine, cover, and cook for 2 to 3 minutes, until spinach is wilted. Stir in crème fraîche, lemon juice, and tarragon and mix well to loosen the crème fraîche and create a luxurious mix of mushrooms and spinach. Bring mushroom broth to a boil on medium-high heat and whisk in cold butter, truffle oil, and chives. Season to taste with salt and pepper.

Halibut Preheat the oven to 350°F. Heat olive oil in a large ovenproof pan on medium-high. Season halibut fillets with salt and add to the pan. Sear fish on one side for 4 to 5 minutes, or until golden brown. Flip, place pan in the oven, and roast for 5 minutes. Add butter to the pan and baste fish for 1 to 2 minutes. Transfer fish to a non-stick baking sheet.

To assemble Set oven to broil.

Place a cut brioche crust on top of each halibut fillet and broil until the crumb begins to brown. Set aside.

Warm tartare sauce until hot but not boiling. Meanwhile, divide mushroom broth among 4 serving plates. Place a fillet on each plate. Stir tartare sauce well and spoon a healthy serving over and around each fillet. Serve immediately.

Chickpea aioli
¼ cup chopped parsley
½ cup tahini
2 Tbsp fresh lemon juice
1 Tbsp kosher salt
2 cloves garlic
2 cups cooked chickpeas
1 cup extra-virgin olive oil

Falafel
½ cup finely chopped parsley
2 Tbsp fresh lemon juice
2 Tbsp kosher salt
2 cloves garlic
2 cups cooked chickpeas
1 Tbsp ground cumin
1½ Tbsp baking soda
1 tsp cayenne
½ tsp ground allspice
4 jalapeños, seeded and roughly
    chopped (optional)
4 green onions, roughly chopped
2 cups oil, for frying

Fried chickpeas
1 cup cooked chickpeas
Salt and freshly ground
    black pepper

 Serves 4

Hearts of Palm Carpaccio with Falafel, Fried Chickpeas, and Za'atar Tomatoes

Chickpea aioli Place all ingredients except olive oil into a food processor and blend until smooth.

Slowly add in olive oil until emulsified. Season to taste with additional lemon juice and salt, if desired. Place mixture into a piping bag and set aside.

Falafel Add all ingredients except oil to a food processor and blend until smooth. Transfer to a bowl and chill in freezer for 20 minutes. Shape into 1½-inch balls.

Heat oil in a saucepan on medium until it reaches 325°F. Working in batches, carefully add falafel and fry for 5 minutes, or until golden brown. Using a slotted spoon, transfer falafel to a plate lined with paper towel. Reserve oil.

Fried chickpeas Using paper towels, pat chickpeas dry. Heat oil reserved from the preparation of the falafels in a saucepan on medium-high until it reaches 300°F. Fry chickpeas for 30 seconds. Using a slotted spoon, transfer chickpeas to a plate lined with paper towel. Season with salt and pepper to taste.

Za'atar tomatoes
30 cherry tomatoes
Extra-virgin olive oil
¼ cup dried oregano
¼ cup sumac
¼ cup ground cumin
4 tsp kosher salt
4 Tbsp toasted sesame seeds

Hearts of palm carpaccio
¼ large zucchini, sliced into thin rounds
⅙ English cucumber, sliced into thin rounds
⅙ heart of palm, sliced into thin rounds
Fresh mint, roughly chopped
Extra-virgin olive oil

 Leftover falafel can be stored in the fridge for up to 3 days. Warm in a 200°F oven and serve in salads or pitas.

Za'atar tomatoes Fill a medium saucepan with at least 6 inches of water and bring to a boil on high heat. Using a paring knife, lightly score an *X* in the bottom of each tomato (later, this will help the skin separate from the flesh). Gently lower tomatoes into the boiling water and blanch for 30 seconds, until the skin cracks. Using a slotted spoon, remove tomatoes from the water and place them immediately in a bowl of ice water. Once cool, remove tomato skins.

Place tomatoes in a bowl and lightly dress with olive oil to coat. In a separate small bowl, combine remaining ingredients and mix well. Sprinkle spice mixture liberally over tomatoes and then place them in a dehydrator overnight. (Alternatively, if you don't have a dehydrator, dehydrate the tomatoes in a 170°F oven for 2 hours.)

Hearts of palm carpaccio Arrange sliced vegetables on 4 plates, creating a mosaic of colour.

To assemble, drizzle chickpea aioli across the plates, streaking it back and forth to cover vegetables. Crumble 2 falafel over each plate and garnish with fried chickpeas and za'atar tomatoes. Top with fresh mint and a drizzle of olive oil.

The Cheese Boutique

Basilio Pesce

THE PRISTINE FAMILY is Toronto cheese royalty: rulers of a sovereign gourmet nation for almost a half-century, they are bound by *affinage*, the art of carefully aging cheese. Afrim Pristine, a maître fromager (one of only about 50 in the world), roams the globe in search of its best cheeses and then makes them even better by further aging them in the on-site cheese cave in the South Kingsway shop. (My heart flutters at the thought of their wheel of Parmigiano that's been aging since 2002.) A happy slice of Europe on a west-side industrial strip, the store is massive, and not an inch of space goes unused. Prosciutto hangs from the ceiling; 30 types of olives are on display; and vinegars, mustards, and jams cram the shelving while fresh pastries and cakes fill the copious display cases. This is party central—not just because the staff routinely hand out espressos as you chat and sample, but also because executive chef Basilio Pesce (formerly of the late, great Porzia) prepares the best muffuletta sandwiches with house-made salumi and cheeses for you to pack up and serve at your soirées. Though at the Cheese Boutique, the party has already begun.

FACING: Squid Ink Corzetti with Mussels and Nduja

Corzetti

4 cups "00" flour, plus extra for dusting

4 cups fine durum semolina

Kosher salt

9 eggs

1 Tbsp extra-virgin olive oil

2 Tbsp squid ink

Parsley

½ cup vegetable oil, for shallow-frying

1 cup flat-leaf parsley leaves, stems removed

Kosher salt

Breadcrumbs

1 Tbsp olive oil

1½ cups breadcrumbs

Kosher salt

 You can make your dough a day ahead. Just allow dough to come to room temperature for 2 hours before rolling.

Corzetti is an embossed coin-shaped pasta traditionally from Liguria in Italy. The pasta is stamped and cut by hand; some stamps are still hand-carved with ornate designs. Stampi corzetti are difficult to find but can be purchased on eBay. You can substitute a good-quality short pasta, like strozzapreti or orecchiette, both of which are available at The Cheese Boutique.

 Serves 4–6

Squid Ink Corzetti with Mussels and Nduja

Corzetti In a large bowl, mix flour and semolina and add a pinch of salt. Form a well in the centre.

In separate bowl, combine eggs, olive oil, and squid ink and mix well. Add egg mixture into the well. Using a fork, slowly incorporate flour from the inside edge of the well into the eggs, mixing well until it forms a thick paste. Using a pastry scraper, fold the rest of the flour into mixture to form a dough. Once eggs are well incorporated, gently knead by folding dough onto itself for 15 to 20 minutes, until it is smooth and shiny. (You cannot over-knead this dough; in fact, the longer you knead, the better.)

Place dough on a well-floured surface, wrap loosely with plastic wrap, and rest for at least 1 hour and up to 2 days. Roll out dough through a pasta roller, reducing the thickness one setting at a time (this avoids stressing the dough) until it's an eighth of an inch thick. Work quickly and, using a *stampi corzetti*, cut and press your coins. Transfer pasta to a well-floured baking sheet and set aside.

Parsley Place vegetable oil in a deep saucepan and heat until it reaches a temperature of 280°F.

Using paper towels, pat dry the parsley leaves and remove as much moisture as possible. Working in batches, add parsley leaves to the pan and gently fry for 20 seconds, or until leaves stop bubbling. (Too much parsley in the hot oil will cause it to splatter.) Using a slotted spoon, transfer parsley onto a plate lined with paper towels. Season to taste with salt and set aside.

Breadcrumbs Heat olive oil in a frying pan on medium. Add breadcrumbs and a few pinches of salt and cook for 8 to 10 minutes, until breadcrumbs are dark but not burnt. Remove from the pan and set aside.

Mussels

2 lbs mussels, cleaned
2 Tbsp extra-virgin olive oil
½ onion, diced
6 cloves garlic, finely chopped
2 bay leaves
1 large sprig fresh thyme
Kosher salt
Pinch of chili flakes
1 cup water
Juice of ½ a lemon

Assembly

10 oz nduja, casings removed (see Tip)
2 Tbsp unsalted butter, chilled
Extra-virgin olive oil
Coarsely ground black pepper

Nduja is a cured, spreadable pork salami from Calabria in Italy. It is traditionally made with pork shoulder, back fat, belly, tripe, peppers, and spices.

Mussels Wash and rinse mussels under cold water and place in a colander to drain.

Heat oil in a large saucepan on medium. Add onions and garlic and sauté for 5 to 7 minutes, until onions are translucent. Add bay leaves and thyme. Season to taste with salt and chili flakes. Add mussels and gently stir until well coated. Add water and lemon juice, cover, and steam for 4 to 6 minutes, until mussels start to open. Remove from the heat and let sit for 3 minutes. Remove mussels and transfer to a baking sheet until they are cold enough to handle. Discard any mussels that have not opened.

Strain liquid from the saucepan and set aside. Remove mussels from the shells and debeard. Add a few spoons of the cooking liquid and cover. Discard shells.

To assemble Break nduja into small bite-size pieces and allow to come to room temperature.

Bring a large pot of salted water to a boil. (Your pasta water should taste like the sea.) Add corzetti and cook for 3 to 5 minutes, until al dente. (The pasta should still have a small amount of "crunch" in the middle.) Drain and set aside.

Heat reserved mussel cooking liquid in a frying pan on medium and cook until reduced by a quarter. Add pasta and cook for another 2 to 3 minutes, until liquid begins to thicken from the pasta starch. Add cooked mussels, nduja, and cold butter and heat until butter is just melted. Finish with a few tablespoons of olive oil.

To serve, arrange pasta on a flat plate to show off the embossed coins. Top with equal amounts of mussels and nduja and some of the pan juice. Drizzle with olive oil and finish with black pepper. Garnish with a tablespoon of breadcrumbs and fried parsley leaves and serve immediately.

Bomba

3 cups red finger chilies

1 cup habanero chilies

2 tsp kosher salt

1 cup red wine vinegar

½ cup granulated sugar

2 fresh bay leaves

1 cup vegetable oil

Muffuletta

1 cup jarred pickled vegetables, such as Roland or Aurora

1 cup green olives in oil, pitted and sliced

6 large panini or preferred bun

24 slices mild provolone

32 oz sliced prosciutto cotto

32 oz sliced spicy sopressata

32 oz sliced mortadella

32 oz sliced Genoa salumi

Bomba, to taste (see here)

 With all the chilies in this recipe, it's essential to wear latex gloves.

 Serves 12

Muffuletta

Bomba Roughly chop chilies (including seeds). Place chilies into a food processor. Making sure not to stand directly over the food processor or inhale the fumes, purée chilies until smooth. Season to taste with salt and set aside in a bowl.

In a saucepan on medium heat, combine vinegar, sugar, and bay leaves and heat until mixture has reduced and lightly caramelized (temperature will be between 300°F and 310°F). Add chili purée—avoid standing directly over the saucepan (the fumes can be intense)—and sauté for 5 to 7 minutes, stirring frequently. Add vegetable oil, reduce heat to medium-low, and simmer for 20 minutes, stirring occasionally. Set aside to cool and then pour into a sterilized jar.

Muffuletta Place pickled vegetables and olives in a food processor and process until coarsely chopped. (Alternatively, chop everything by hand.) Set aside.

Cut each panini in half and separate top from bottom. Spread 2 to 3 Tbsp of olive mixture onto each bottom half. Starting from the bottom up, arrange as evenly as possible: 4 slices provolone, 8 slices prosciutto cotto, 10 slices sopressata, 5 slices mortadella, and 10 slices Genoa salumi. Spread a small amount of bomba across the top half of each panini. (Add more bomba if you prefer a spicier sandwich.) Place top bun over the sandwich and give a good press. Cut each muffuletta in half and serve immediately.

Community Food Centres Canada

Nick Saul

IF YOU'RE READING this book, you already know how transformative food can be. Few understand this better than Nick Saul, president and chief executive officer of Community Food Centres Canada (CFCC). I first met Saul at a Chefs for Change dinner, held each winter over several weeks in Toronto, where the country's best like-minded chefs volunteer their time and cook together to raise money to create and sustain more Community Food Centres. "We need more chefs, more restaurants, more home cooks, and more caring Canadians to join our movement for a healthier and more equitable food system— and country," says Saul. "Food connects us."

CFCC builds and supports vibrant and dignified food-focused spaces in low-income communities across Canada, "where people come together to grow, cook, share, and advocate for good food for all." They also work together to push for public policies that put health, community, and equality first. Because access to good food is a basic human right.

FACING: Black Bean and Sweet Potato Tacos

Bean and sweet potato filling

1 sweet potato, chopped into
   1-inch cubes

4 Tbsp extra-virgin olive oil
   or coconut oil, divided

½ tsp nutmeg

1 onion, diced

2 cloves garlic, minced

¼ tsp ground cinnamon

1 tsp ground cumin

2 tsp ancho chili powder

2 cups canned black beans,
   drained and rinsed

4 Roma tomatoes, broiled until
   blistered, then peeled and diced

¼ cup water

Tomato salsa

5 Roma tomatoes

1 clove garlic, minced

2 tsp extra-virgin olive oil

1–2 serrano chilies, seeded and diced

2 tsp fresh lime juice

2 Tbsp chopped cilantro (optional)

Salt and freshly ground pepper

 Serves 4

Black Bean and Sweet Potato Tacos

Black bean and sweet potato filling Preheat the oven to 425°F.

Spread sweet potatoes on a baking sheet, drizzle with 1 Tbsp olive oil, and toss. Sprinkle with nutmeg and roast for 10 minutes. Turn potatoes and roast for another 10 minutes. Remove from the oven and set aside.

Heat the remaining 3 Tbsp of olive oil in a large frying pan on medium. Add onions and sauté for 5 minutes. Add garlic and sauté for another minute, until fragrant and the onions are translucent. Add cinnamon, cumin, and chili powder and stir to incorporate.

Add black beans, tomatoes, and water to the pan and stir until well mixed. Reduce heat to medium-low and cook, uncovered, for another 5 minutes. Using the back of a slotted spoon, mash the beans as you stir, leaving roughly half of the beans whole. Reduce heat to low and set aside while you prepare the salsas.

Tomato salsa Fill a medium saucepan with at least 6 inches of water and bring to a boil on high heat. Using a paring knife, lightly score an *X* in the bottom of each tomato (later, this will help the skin separate from the flesh). Gently lower tomatoes into the boiling water and blanch for 30 seconds, until the skin cracks. Using a slotted spoon, remove tomatoes from the water and place them immediately in a bowl of ice water. Once cool, remove tomato skins.

Cut tomatoes in half, top to bottom, and remove the seeds. Cut tomatoes into a rough dice and place in a stainless steel or glass bowl. Toss with remaining ingredients and set aside.

White nectarine salsa

4 white nectarines

2-inch piece fresh ginger, grated

1–2 tsp diced jalapeño

Juice of 1 small lime

½ tsp sweet paprika

Salt

Assembly

12 fresh corn tortillas (6 inch)

9 oz queso fresco or feta

¼ cup cilantro (optional)

White nectarine salsa Fill a medium saucepan with at least 6 inches of water and bring to a boil on high heat. Using a paring knife, lightly score an *X* into the bottom of each nectarine (later, this will help the skin separate from the flesh). Gently lower nectarines into the boiling water and blanch for 60 seconds, until the skin cracks. Using a slotted spoon, remove nectarines from the water and place immediately in a bowl of ice water. Once cool, remove skins and chop nectarines.

Gather grated ginger in your hand and squeeze it tightly over the bowl of nectarines to extract the juice. Discard ginger pulp. Toss nectarines with the remaining ingredients, adjusting salt to taste.

To assemble In a frying pan set on medium-high heat, warm tortillas for 1 minute on each side. Plate warmed tortillas and fill with black beans, sweet potatoes, and queso fresco or feta. Top with salsas and cilantro (if using) and serve.

Meringue

1½ cups ground pistachios
  (see Tip)

2 Tbsp cornstarch

1 cup + 6 Tbsp granulated
  sugar, divided

6 egg whites, room temperature

Ground pistachio can be purchased from specialty food stores. If you prefer to make it at home, bring a pot of water to a boil on high heat, add pistachios, and blanch for 1 to 2 minutes, or until the peels begin to lift off the nuts. Strain nuts and transfer them to a bowl of ice water. Drain and peel pistachios by hand (use a kitchen towel to loosen skins even more). Transfer peeled pistachios to a blender or food processor and blend until desired consistency is achieved.

 Serves 8–10

Celebration Cake

Meringue Preheat the oven to 250°F.

Line 3 baking sheets with parchment paper and draw an 8-inch circle on each paper. (Alternatively, flip over a cake pan onto parchment paper and trace). Set aside.

In a medium bowl, combine ground pistachios, cornstarch, and 1 cup of sugar. Mix well.

In a large bowl or stand mixer, whip egg whites until stiff. Add remaining 6 Tbsp sugar and whip for another 30 seconds, until whites appear glossy and the meringue holds peaks. Fold pistachio mixture, in three batches, into the meringue.

Gently fill a pastry bag with the meringue (a freezer bag is an adequate substitute) and pipe a disk onto the parchment paper, starting at the centre of the circle and stopping at the edgings. Repeat with the other two.

Bake for 50 to 60 minutes, until crisp, dry, and light brown. Turn off oven and leave meringue to dry.

Buttercream
½ cup granulated sugar
6 Tbsp water
4 egg yolks
1 cup unsalted butter, room
    temperature
1½ tsp rosewater

Assembly
½ cup chopped pistachios,
    plus extra for garnish
7 oz honeycomb, chopped
    into 1-inch pieces

 For a lighter-tasting cake, use only half of the buttercream and ice with lightly sweetened whipped cream.

Buttercream In a small saucepan on medium-high heat, dissolve sugar in water. Bring mixture to a boil until the syrup reaches soft ball stage (235°F). (When you drop a bit of the syrup into cold water to test it, it will form a soft ball.) Do not stir.

In a large bowl, whisk egg yolks with a hand mixer. Gradually pour the hot syrup into yolks, whisking continuously to prevent yolks from scrambling. Beat mixture as quickly as possible for another 5 minutes. The mixture should cool and form a thick, uniform mousse. Allow to cool.

In a small bowl, cream butter, then add to yolk mixture. Stir in rose water.

To assemble Place one layer of meringue on a serving plate. Spread a quarter of the buttercream on the meringue, add a second layer of meringue, and cover with another quarter of buttercream. Place the final meringue on top and cover the top and sides with the remaining buttercream.

Press chopped pistachios around the top edge of the cake, then refrigerate for at least 2 hours. Remove cake from the fridge. Mound pieces of honeycomb on top of the cake and sprinkle with additional chopped pistachios.

DaiLo
Nick Liu

CHEF NICK LIU calls his food "New Asian"; I call it straight up addictive. Liu intrinsically knows what people want to eat, and he satisfies those cravings by imagining lip-smacking dishes such as fried watermelon and truffle fried rice. Scaramouche, Splendido, and Niagara Street Café were the backbone of Liu's training, but he also worked abroad in Italy, England, and Australia. With fresh inspiration, he returned to Toronto several years ago and opened DaiLo with sommelier Anton Potvin, creating the most convivial dining experience this side of the moon. Teeming with bold Far East flavours and Parisian flair, a meal at the restaurant is a time-travelling taste experience in an *Orient-Express*-meets-College-Street room.

I visit often to enjoy favourites like pumpkin dumplings and the whole fried Giggie trout, plus the specials that often make their way onto the main menu. Liu mentors his chefs, and part of that training includes recipe development challenges focused on a single ingredient, like rhubarb. To that end, there are Ontario pea dumplings with smoked Chinese sausage and soy brown butter, spoon-tender sweet-and-sour pork hock, and the mainstay that are his grandfather's Hakka brown wontons with house XO sauce. For inspired cocktails and a Big Mac bao, don't forget to visit their LoPan bar upstairs.

FACING: Peking Glazed Duck Breast with Asian Bread Stuffing and Mandarin Cranberry Sauce

Asian bread stuffing

½ loaf egg bread, cut into 1-inch cubes

1 cup butter

1 onion, diced

3 cloves garlic, minced

10 shiitake mushroom, sliced

3–4 Chinese sausages, sliced into
    rounds (see Tip)

1 Tbsp chopped fresh sage leaves

2 Tbsp chopped cilantro

Salt and freshly ground black pepper

Mandarin cranberry sauce

2 mandarin oranges

2 Tbsp orange juice

2 Tbsp port

1 cup granulated sugar

1 Tbsp water

1 tsp light corn syrup

2 cups frozen cranberries

2 star anise

Salt and freshly ground black pepper

 Chef Liu smokes his Chinese sausage first to give the stuffing a nice smoky accent. If you have access to a smoker, he highly recommends it.

 Serves 4

Peking Glazed Duck Breast with Asian Bread Stuffing and Mandarin Cranberry Sauce

Asian bread stuffing Preheat the oven to 400°F. Place bread on a baking sheet and toast for 3 to 5 minutes, or until golden brown. Remove from the oven and set aside.

In a large pot on medium heat, melt butter. Add onions and garlic and sauté for 1 to 2 minutes. Add mushrooms, sausage, and sage and cook for another 3 to 5 minutes. Add toasted bread to the pot, stir, and cook on medium heat for 5 minutes, or until bread is soft. Remove from the heat and stir in cilantro. Taste and adjust seasoning with salt and pepper, if needed. (Because salted butter is used in this recipe, it may not need extra salt.) Cover and set aside.

Mandarin cranberry sauce Using a vegetable peeler, peel the zest of the mandarins and cut into short, thin strips. Set aside. Cut mandarins in half, squeeze juice into a bowl, and discard pith. Add orange juice and port to the bowl, stir, and set aside.

Place sugar in a heavy-bottomed saucepan and drizzle in water and light corn syrup. (The corn syrup prevents the sugar from forming hard crystals.) Turn the heat to medium-high and stir sugar until it begins to melt. Allow sugar to boil. Do not touch or stir for 7 to 10 minutes, or until it starts to turn light amber. (If you feel the need to move the contents of the saucepan, gently swirl it.) Add cranberries and star anise, swirling them in the caramel. (The caramel is very hot, so be careful not to burn yourself.) When the cranberries begin to burst, remove the saucepan from the heat and pour in the juice mixture around the sides of the pan. Stir with a wooden spoon or silicone spatula to incorporate everything into mixture.

Peking duck breast

2 King Cole duck breasts

5 Tbsp sesame oil, divided

1 Tbsp five-spice powder

Salt and freshly ground black pepper

1 clove garlic, crushed

3 sprigs fresh thyme

1 Tbsp unsalted butter

2 Tbsp sweet soy sauce

Add mandarin zest to the saucepan, and salt and pepper to taste. Return the saucepan to the stove and simmer on low heat for 5 to 10 minutes, or until thickened. The compote will thicken when cooled, so try not to overcook it. Transfer to a heat-resistant container and cool to room temperature. Set aside until you're ready for assembly.

Peking duck breast Coat duck breasts with 2 Tbsp sesame oil and rub with five-spice powder, salt, and pepper. Air-dry the duck in the fridge for 2 hours. (The skin will be crispier when cooked.)

Heat the remaining 3 Tbsp of sesame oil in a cast-iron pan on high. Place duck breasts, skin-side up, in the pan and sear for 2 minutes, or until golden brown. Using tongs, flip the breasts over on to their skin and reduce heat to medium-high. Add garlic, thyme, and butter. Sear for 5 minutes, basting every minute, until skin is golden brown and crispy. Remove duck from the pan and set aside to rest for 5 minutes. Using a pastry brush, glaze with sweet soy sauce.

Thinly slice duck breasts with a sharp knife and fan out on a serving platter. Ladle sauce into a ramekin and place on the platter (or drizzle over the dish, if desired). Serve with a side of Asian bread stuffing and mandarin cranberry sauce and enjoy.

Pumpkin dumplings

1 pumpkin or Kabocha squash
2 Tbsp vegetable oil
½ cup brown sugar, divided
1 Tbsp salt
2 cloves garlic, thinly sliced
½-inch piece fresh ginger, thinly sliced
3 sprigs fresh thyme
2 Tbsp rice vinegar
20 wonton skins
1 egg, lightly beaten

Brown butter soy sauce

1 cup unsalted butter
1 cup whipping (35%) cream
2 Tbsp soy sauce

 Serves 4

Pumpkin Dumplings with Brown Butter Soy, Truffles, Almond Crumble, and White Rabbit Candy Glaze

Pumpkin dumplings Preheat the oven to 425°F. Cut pumpkin or squash in half and scoop out seeds. Drizzle oil on both fleshy halves and sprinkle with 3 Tbsp brown sugar, salt, garlic, ginger, and thyme. Place on a baking sheet skin-side down and bake for 1 hour, or until flesh is soft and caramelized.

Discard ginger and thyme, scoop out flesh, and place in a food processor. Add rice vinegar and purée until smooth. Taste and season with additional salt and brown sugar if necessary.

On a clean surface, set out 5 wonton skins. Place 1 Tbsp of purée in the centre of each skin. Brush two edges of the wonton skins with egg and fold over to create a triangle. Press along the edges with your fingers to seal each dumpling. Brush a small amount of egg wash on one of the corners and connect two corners, sealing them to form

a tortellini-style dumpling. Repeat process with remaining wonton skins. Keep dumplings in the fridge or freezer until assembly.

Brown butter soy sauce In a small saucepan on high heat, melt butter. Reduce heat to medium-low, wait until butter splits, and cook until milk solids turn golden brown. Whisk the bottom of the pan frequently to scrape off any toasted milk solids. (Be careful not to burn your butter.)

Remove saucepan from the heat and set aside to cool slightly. Add cream and soy sauce while mixing well to make sure the sauce emulsifies. Put aside until assembly.

White Rabbit candy glaze
8 White Rabbit candies
½ cup whipping (35%) cream

Assembly
Zest and juice of 1 lemon
¼ cup toasted almonds, crushed
    to a crumble
2 Tbsp truffle oil
1 green onion, thinly sliced
1 red chili, thinly sliced
¼ cup cilantro leaves, stems removed
1 fresh black truffle

White Rabbit candy glaze Place candies and cream in a small saucepan and cook on medium heat for 5 minutes, until candy has melted and thickened into a thin glaze.

To assemble Bring a pot of water to a boil, add dumplings, and cook for 4 minutes, or until they start to float. Meanwhile, in a saucepan, heat brown butter sauce, making sure it stays emulsified. (Tip: Heat a tablespoon of cream in your pan before adding brown butter sauce to prevent sauce from splitting.) Drain dumplings and add them to the saucepan with 2 Tbsp of cooking water. Toss and cook until sauce thickens slightly. Add a squeeze of lemon juice to adjust the acid balance.

Place 5 dumplings on each plate along with some of the sauce. Drizzle a small amount of White Rabbit candy glaze over the dumplings. Sprinkle with almond crumble, drizzle with truffle oil, and garnish with green onion, red chili, and cilantro. Sprinkle a little lemon zest over the dumplings and finish with shavings of black truffle.

David H. Chow Chocolates & Confections

David H. Chow

ANYONE WHO DOESN'T love artisanal hand-crafted chocolate is no friend of mine. David Chow made a name for himself as executive pastry chef at the Drake Hotel (they'll never remove his blueberry scones from the menu) before striking out on his own with an eponymous collection of high-quality products, made from Valronha chocolate and Ontario-grown goods. The offerings change with the seasons but include sweets such as yuzu caramels and a dark chocolate bar laced with salted caramel and infused with wildflower honey, fresh rosemary, and Maldon salt. "Infusing a classic salted butter caramel sauce with local honey and the resinous notes of fresh rosemary definitely brings it to the next level," says Chow. The recipe

for that sauce is in this book, and is often part of Chow's multifaceted desserts, the building blocks for which shine all on their own. In fact, he says his favourite way to enjoy the caramel sauce (besides eating it directly from the jar) is warmed and drizzled over a pan of fudgy brownie batter that, when popped into the oven, transforms into "the most delectable caramel swirl brownies ever."

FACING: Dark Chocolate Cherry Tart with White Chocolate Ganache

Whipped white chocolate ganache

1¼ cups chopped high-quality white chocolate, such as Valrhona Opalys

2 cups whipping (35%) cream, divided

2 Tbsp liquid glucose or corn syrup

2 Tbsp good-quality Ontario honey

1 tsp finely grated tonka bean, vanilla paste, or vanilla extract

⅛ tsp kosher salt

Dark chocolate filling

1¼ cups chopped high-quality dark chocolate (64% cocoa) such as Valrhona Manjari

½ cup granulated sugar

6½ Tbsp cacao powder

½ tsp kosher salt

1 cup whipping (35%) cream

1 cup whole milk

4 egg yolks

 Makes 12 (3½-inch) tarts or 2 (8-inch) fluted tarts

Dark Chocolate Cherry Tart with White Chocolate Ganache

Whipped white chocolate ganache In a bowl set over a pot of barely simmering water, melt the chocolate.

Meanwhile, in a heavy-bottomed saucepan on medium-high heat, combine ⅔ cup of cream, glucose or corn syrup, honey, tonka bean or vanilla paste or extract, and salt and bring to a boil. Slowly drizzle the hot cream mixture into the melted chocolate, whisking continuously to create a smooth and silky ganache. (Alternatively, use an immersion blender.) Whisk in the remaining 1⅓ cups cream and stir well to combine.

Pour mixture into a container, cover, and chill in the fridge for at least 8 hours, but ideally overnight.

Dark chocolate filling In a bowl set over a pot of barely simmering water, melt chocolate.

Meanwhile, in a heavy-bottomed saucepan on medium-high heat, combine sugar, cacao powder, and salt, add cream and milk, and bring mixture to a boil. Whisk continuously to remove lumps.

Slowly drizzle the hot cream mixture into the melted chocolate, whisking continuously until the chocolate has completely dissolved and emulsified with the liquid. (Alternatively, use an immersion blender.) Chill mixture quickly over an ice bath until cooled. Stir in egg yolks until thoroughly mixed, and then refrigerate, covered, for at least 8 hours or overnight.

Chocolate tart dough

1¾ cups unsalted butter, room temperature
1 cup granulated sugar
8 egg yolks
½ tsp kosher salt
4 cups + 2 Tbsp all-purpose flour
¾ cup cacao powder

Assembly

4 cups Morello cherries, pitted
Icing sugar, for dusting (optional)
Chocolate shavings (optional)

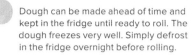

Dough can be made ahead of time and kept in the fridge until ready to roll. The dough freezes very well. Simply defrost in the fridge overnight before rolling.

Make the tart ahead of time during the day, let it cool to room temperature, and, at the last minute, garnish with whipped cream, shards or shavings of dark chocolate, fresh whole cherries, and caramelized cacao nibs for extra crunch. Perfect to impress dinner party or potluck guests.

If you're on a gluten-free diet or need a dessert in a pinch, you can forgo the tart shells and bake the cherries and chocolate filling in a beautiful casserole or heavy cast-iron pan. It can be done with any fruit, but good choices are pears, raspberries, and figs.

Chocolate tart dough Using a stand mixer fitted with the paddle attachment, cream together butter and sugar. Add egg yolks one at a time until incorporated, scraping the bowl with a spatula between each addition.

In a separate bowl, combine dry ingredients and mix well, then add to the wet mixture. Mix on low speed until just combined.

Place dough on a large piece of plastic wrap and flatten into a disk. Wrap tightly and refrigerate for at least 1 hour, or until firm. Unwrap dough, roll it to a ¼-inch thickness, and line twelve 3½-inch or two 8-inch tart pans with the dough. (Pans with removable bases are recommended.) Place tart shells in the fridge and chill for 1 hour.

Preheat the oven to 350°F. Line tart shells with a round of parchment paper and fill with pie weights or baking beans. Par-bake for 12 to 15 minutes, until set but still slightly soft when touched. (They won't be completely done, as they'll be baked again with the filling). Remove the parchment paper and pie weights or beans.

To assemble Fill tart shells with cherries. Stir chilled chocolate mixture and pour over cherries until shells are filled completely. If using small tart pans, bake in 350°F oven for 12 to 15 minutes, or until mixture is set and no longer wobbles in the centre. If using large tart pans, bake for 25 to 35 minutes. Set aside to cool until barely warm.

To serve, place white chocolate ganache into the bowl of a stand mixer fitted with the whisk attachment and whip until it holds soft peaks (do not over-whip). Dust icing sugar over tarts or sprinkle with chocolate shavings, as desired, and allow guests to dollop ganache directly onto the warm tarts.

1½ cups whipping (35%) cream

2 sprigs fresh rosemary

1 cup water

2 cups granulated sugar

½ cup Rosewood Estates or any light honey (see Tip)

2 Tbsp liquid glucose or corn syrup (optional)

½ cup butter, chilled (see Tip)

 Avoid dark honeys such as buckwheat or chestnut honey—the flavour may be too strong and will overwhelm the sauce.

If you're limiting your sodium intake, you can use unsalted butter and up to ¾ tsp kosher salt. Please don't leave the salt out—it's what balances the sauce.

VARIATIONS: Variations can be made by using thyme, bay leaves, or even a single habanero chili. Instead of using herbs, infuse cream with Earl Grey tea, coffee beans, vanilla, and tonka bean, or add a tablespoon or two of your favourite bourbon.

 **Makes 2½ cups**

Salted Honey and Rosemary Caramel Sauce

In a small, heavy-bottomed saucepan, bring cream and rosemary to a boil on medium-high heat. Remove the pot from the heat immediately, cover, and set aside to infuse for 15 minutes.

Place water, sugar, honey, and glucose (if using) into another heavy-bottomed pot on medium heat and stir until nearly all of the sugar is dissolved. Increase heat to high and cook for 10 minutes, without stirring, until mixture turns a light amber brown or reaches 350°F on a candy thermometer. (Once the liquid begins to change colour and caramelize, keep a watchful eye on it while swirling the pan—it will go from a light caramel to burnt very quickly.)

Remove the pan from the heat and whisk in butter. (Be careful, as mixture is very hot.) Whisking continuously, slowly drizzle the rosemary-infused cream into the pan. Stir until you get a smooth caramel sauce. To remove any lumps, simply warm mixture on medium heat until they melt into the sauce.

Strain sauce into a sterilized glass jar and allow to cool before using. Discard rosemary and any remaining lumps. The sauce will keep covered in a glass jar in the fridge for 1 month. (If the caramel is too thick to use directly from the fridge, simply set it in a container of hot water or warm it up briefly in the microwave.)

Delica Kitchen
Graham Bower and Devin Connell

WALKING OFF OF Yonge Street and into this bakery café, you get the feeling that you've swanned onto a Nancy Myer film set: white clapboard walls, polished wood, and fresh flowers. But founder and co-owner Devin Connell—who shares mind and palate with chef Graham Bower—comes by this high style honestly: she holds a graphic design degree from Parsons School of Design in New York, an Art Business certificate from Sotheby's Institute in London (U.K.), and a certificate of Fine Pastry Techniques from Le Cordon Bleu in Paris. Great, now I feel bad about myself. Good thing there are loads of decadent treats

here to make me feel better, including the famous jammies. "They've been on the menu since we opened," says Connell. "We consider them one of our signature items, and there might be riots if we ever took them off." What's a jammy? "The best way to describe this treat is part scone, part doughnut, part strawberry shortcake: a trifecta of deliciousness," she says. The good news? The recipe is in this book.

Turkey chili

1 red pepper

2 Tbsp canola oil

2 lbs ground turkey

1 yellow onion, diced

3 cloves garlic, minced

1 jalapeño pepper, seeded
and minced

1 can (28 oz) whole San
Marzano tomatoes, puréed

1 can (19 oz) black beans,
drained and rinsed

1 can (19 oz) red kidney
beans, drained and rinsed

¼ cup Worcestershire sauce

2 Tbsp tomato paste

2 Tbsp molasses

3 tsp chili powder

2 tsp cumin

1 tsp mustard powder

1 tsp kosher salt

½ tsp dried oregano

½ tsp dried basil

¼ tsp cayenne

Assembly

2 Tbsp unsalted butter

4 slices cornbread, cut into
1-inch cubes

1 cup sour cream

2 Tbsp smoked paprika

¼ cup chives, minced

 Serves 6

Turkey Chili with Cornbread Croutons and Chive Sour Cream

Turkey chili Preheat a grill or broiler and char the pepper for 2 to 3 minutes per side, or until almost black. Place pepper in a bowl, wrap tightly with plastic wrap, and set aside for 15 minutes. Peel, seed, and chop.

Heat canola oil in a large pot set on medium until just smoking, then add turkey and onions and cook for 7 minutes, or until onions are translucent and the meat is cooked. Add garlic and jalapeño and sauté for another 2 minutes.

Add remaining ingredients and mix well. (Make sure nothing is sticking to the bottom of the pot.) Reduce heat to medium-low, cover, and cook for 1½ hours.

To assemble When ready to serve, melt butter in a frying pan on medium-high heat and add cornbread. Fry for 2 to 3 minutes, until browned. Transfer to a bowl and set aside.

In a small bowl, combine sour cream, smoked paprika, and chives and mix well.

Ladle chili into individual serving bowls, top with a dollop of chive sour cream, and garnish with cornbread croutons.

Unsalted butter, room
temperature, for greasing

All-purpose flour, for dusting

1 cup cream cheese, room
temperature

½ cup unsalted butter,
room temperature

2 eggs, lightly beaten

¼ cup whole milk

2 tsp vanilla extract

½ tsp almond extract

2¼ cups all-purpose flour

1 tsp baking powder

½ tsp baking soda

¼ tsp ground cinnamon

¼ tsp kosher salt

1 cup + 2 Tbsp granulated sugar

1 cup good-quality
strawberry jam

Icing sugar, for dusting

 Makes 24

Delica Kitchen's Strawberry Jammies

Preheat the oven to 375°F. Brush muffin top tins (available at kitchen supply stores) with butter, dust with flour, and set aside.

In the bowl of a stand mixer, combine cream cheese and butter and beat for 3 to 4 minutes. Add eggs, milk, and vanilla and almond extracts and mix well until combined.

In a separate bowl, sift together flour, baking powder, baking soda, cinnamon, salt, and sugar. Add to the wet ingredients and mix on low speed until just combined. Do not overmix.

Scoop a ¼ cup of batter into each mould. Wet your thumb and create a well in the centre of each dough ball. Do not flatten the batter.

Place 2 tsp of jam into the centre of each jammy and swirl through the batter using a paring knife. Bake for 20 to 25 minutes or until golden brown. Remove jammies from the pan while they are still warm and place on a wire rack. Once cooled, dust with icing sugar and serve.

The Espresso Institute of North America

Ezra Braves

THE NATURAL EVOLUTION of Ezra Braves's obsession for all things coffee was to spread the gospel to others. To this end, you may find yourself trekking down a back alley and into a rustic outbuilding in a residential neighbourhood in St. Clair West, and into a large lofty room that can best be described as an upmarket man cave. There's a laboratory of grinders, espresso machines, and percolators, plus electric guitars and a vintage BMW motorcycle for good measure. "The space is great because we can see clients, and jam when we feel like it," jokes the café owner. This is where Braves takes coffee seriously, giving private lessons to both aficionados and café owners so that they, too, can achieve bean bliss. He's helped open dozens of cafés around the city and also makes house calls. Working with professional equipment, clients learn about coffee blending and roasting, grinding for various types of machines, and even latte art. Braves also takes his baked goods seriously—proof can be found and nibbled on at Ezra's Pound, the popular café on Dupont Street. Bake a batch of Sierra's Insanely Awesome Brownies and you'll agree.

¼ lb high-quality coarse ground
  coffee (see Tip)
7½–8 cups cold water

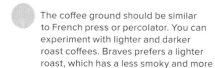

The coffee ground should be similar
to French press or percolator. You can
experiment with lighter and darker
roast coffees. Braves prefers a lighter
roast, which has a less smoky and more
nuanced taste.

 Serves 6–8

Cold Brew

In a pot, glass jar, or any container you prefer, combine cold water and ground coffee and give it a good stir. Place the container in the fridge and set aside for 14 to 16 hours. (Be careful not to brew the coffee too long or you'll have too many coffee solids, resulting is a less delicate taste.)

To filter, pour coffee through a cheesecloth or a paper filter (the paper filter takes longer) and serve over ice or straight up. It can be refrigerated for up to 4 days, or until you notice a slightly sour taste. If you have any leftover coffee, you can pour it into an ice cube tray and freeze; when the cubes melt, your coffee won't be diluted.

1 lb dark chocolate (use 70% for an intense chocolate hit)

2 cups unsalted butter

¼ tsp salt

1¼ cup cocoa powder, sifted

1 cup high-quality organic pastry flour, sifted

5 eggs

3 cups granulated sugar

Flaked sea salt or kosher salt

Coarsely ground coffee beans

 **Makes 24 brownies**

Sierra's Insanely Awesome Brownies

Preheat the oven to 350°F. Spray a 9 × 13-inch rectangular pan with non-stick spray and line with parchment paper. In a double boiler, or a bowl set over simmering water, melt chocolate, butter, and salt and mix with a wooden spoon until well mixed. Set aside to cool.

In a medium bowl, combine cocoa and flour. In a second medium bowl, whisk together eggs and sugar until pale and fluffy. Fold chocolate mixture into egg mixture until combined, then fold in flour mixture. Pour batter into the pan and spread out with a spatula.

Bake for 35 to 45 minutes, until the top forms a crust. Garnish with flaked salt or kosher salt and crushed coffee beans.

FACING: Sierra's Insanely Awesome Brownies, with Cold Brew

Figo

Anna Chen

LUSCIOUS HANDMADE PASTAS and wood-fired pizzas in the heart of the Entertainment District? That's Figo. Diminutive yet commanding, with a penchant for putting original touches on Italian classics? That's Anna Chen. The chef, who worked as a pasta chef at Scaramouche, Zucca, and Buca Yorkville (in other words, the city's best) before taking the helm here, hasn't compromised her perfectionist pasta ways for the party set. Nor did owners Hanif Harji and Charles Khabouth spare any expense with the glossy décor. This is how you do scenester Italian. Designed by Studio Munge, the spacious surrounds are a wash of pastels, custom millwork, and polished concrete. It's very Miami-meets-Milan, as is the menu.

Ricotta, made using a hundred-year-old recipe, is topped with truffle honey and a grinding of black pepper. There's flat-out delicious mussels with fregula, saffron, and tomato, while feather-thin slices of zucchini—fried into *fritti*, piled high, and drizzled with lemon *crema fresca* and honey—are a beautiful thing, both market-fresh and upmarket. Bucatini with juniper-spiced wild boar ragout is the definition of earthy satisfaction, while a delicately charred pizza topped with soppressata, mozzarella, and honey is all sweet heat. And come to think of it, so is Chef Chen.

Saffron tomato sauce
1 Tbsp olive oil
1 red chili, sliced lengthwise, seeded, and cut into ½-inch pieces
1 small fennel bulb, diced
2 small shallots, diced
1 cup white wine
2 cups canned tomatoes
¼ tsp saffron threads
Salt and freshly ground black pepper

Fregula
1 cup dried fregula

Mussels
¼ cup olive oil
1 clove garlic, thinly sliced
½ lb fresh mussels, scrubbed and rinsed
½ cup white wine
Salt and freshly ground black pepper

Assembly
¼ cup croutons, for garnish
1 Tbsp chopped parsley, for garnish
Extra-virgin olive oil
1 lemon, wedged, to serve

 Serves 4

Mussels and Fregula with Saffron Tomato Sauce

Saffron tomato sauce Heat oil in a saucepan on medium. Add chili, fennel, and shallots, and cook for 10 minutes, until browned. Add white wine and simmer for 2 to 3 minutes. Add tomatoes and saffron, reduce heat to medium-low, and season to taste. Simmer for 30 minutes, then transfer sauce to a food processor or blender and blend until smooth. Strain.

Fregula Bring a pot of water to a boil, add fregula, and cook for about 6 minutes, or according to the package instructions, until al dente. Drain and set aside.

Mussels Heat oil in a large frying pan on medium. Add garlic and cook for 30 seconds, or until fragrant. Add mussels and wine, cover, and increase heat to medium-high. Cook for 2 to 3 minutes, until mussels open. Remove from the heat and discard any mussels that have not opened. Season with salt and pepper. Transfer mussels to a bowl.

To assemble When ready to serve, heat saffron tomato sauce in a small saucepan and add fregula. Pour sauce over mussels, garnish with croutons and parsley, and drizzle with olive oil. Serve each dish with a wedge of lemon on the side.

Ricotta

4½ cups whole milk
½ cup whipping (35%) cream
1¼ tsp salt
½ tsp granulated sugar
½ cup water
4 tsp white vinegar
2 tsp fresh lemon juice

Assembly

Salt and freshly ground black
   pepper
½ tsp truffle honey
Good-quality extra-virgin olive
   oil, for drizzling
Crostini

 Makes 4 cups

Ricotta with Truffle Honey

Ricotta In a large heavy-bottomed stainless steel pot on low heat, combine milk, cream, salt, and sugar, stirring gently with a rubber spatula. Meanwhile, line a strainer with cheesecloth and place it over a metal bowl.

In a separate saucepan on high heat, combine water, vinegar, and lemon juice and bring to a boil, then set aside.

Stir milk mixture, increase heat to medium-low, and cook for 45 to 60 minutes, or until the temperature of mixture reaches 210°F. Turn the heat off, add vinegar mixture, and stir gently for a few seconds, until ricotta and whey separate. Strain ricotta through the lined strainer, transfer to a container, and set aside to cool. Refrigerate.

To assemble Place ricotta in a small serving bowl. Season with salt and pepper, drizzle with truffle honey and olive oil, and serve with crostini.

Flock Rotisserie and Greens

Cory Vitiello

CORY VITIELLO, CHEF and owner of the late, great Harbord Room, has opened another instant hit, which features two enduring trends in one handsome spot: take-out gourmet salads *and* rotisserie chicken. With four locations in the works, it's a concept that works. Gleaming French Rotisol rotisseries spin naturally raised chickens with crisped skin, which you should choose to side with sweet potato chunks cooked in the schmaltz drippings and chili-lime salt. But back to those salads. The Boho Flock is a great example of a kitchen-sink winner: marinated kale, red quinoa, roasted and raw beets, currants, pumpkin seeds, pomegranate, vinaigrette, and more—texture, flavour, freshness, zing. A nourishing chicken soup is also on offer, as well as pulled rotisserie sandwiches with crunchy lettuce and avocado on soft milk buns. The Harbord Street location—with the beautiful room and its marble-topped bar and leather booths as well as a patio—is a more elaborate sit-down affair rather than a grab-and-go deal and features the likes of a fried chicken platter and mac and cheese on the menu. But kudos to Vitiello for giving Torontonians hearty and healthy options, done with such care. It's nice to feel good about what you've eaten, even when it happens to be a killer lime tart for dessert.

Meringue
4 egg whites
2 cups icing sugar

Crust
1½ cups graham cracker crumbs
½ cup shredded raw coconut
6 Tbsp melted butter

Lime curd
1 cup granulated sugar
Zest of 5 limes, finely grated
4 eggs
¾ cup fresh lime juice
1¼ cups unsalted butter, cold
    and cut into ½-inch cubes

 The meringue can be made the day before and stored in a tightly sealed container.

Assembly
1 cup whipped (35%) cream
1 lime
Chopped fresh mint
Toasted coconut

 Serves 8

Flock Lime Tart with Coconut and Graham Crust, Cream, and Toasted Meringue

Meringue Preheat the oven to 200°F and line a baking sheet with parchment paper.

Place egg whites in a bowl and, using an electric mixer, beat on high speed until light and frothy. Add sugar, a little at a time, while continuing to whisk until glossy and stiff peaks form.

Spread mixture evenly on the prepared baking sheet and bake for 3 hours, or until dry and toasted. Once meringue is crisp and dry, prop open the oven door with a wooden spoon so moisture can escape. Turn the broiler on and cook for another 2 to 3 minutes, until the top has browned. Let meringue cool down to room temperature.

Crust Preheat the oven to 350°F. In a medium bowl, combine all ingredients and mix until crust comes together and a ball is formed. Evenly spread mixture into a tart shell and, using your fingers, press down to even out the crust and shape it up the sides. Bake for 10 to 15 minutes, or until golden brown. Set aside to cool.

Lime curd In a large stainless steel bowl, combine sugar and lime zest and rub with your fingers until mixture resembles wet sand and is fragrant of lime. Add eggs and lime juice and whisk until well combined.

Place the stainless bowl over a large pot of simmering water and stir with a wooden spoon for 15 minutes, or until thick and silky and the temperature has reached 180°F. Remove the bowl from the heat and set aside for 20 minutes to cool.

Pour curd into a blender, cover, and blend on medium-high speed. Add cold butter in small amounts and blend until fully incorporated. Repeat until all of the butter is used.

Pour curd into baked tart shell and fill to the brim. Refrigerate tart for 2 to 3 hours, until completely chilled. (Alternatively, the tart can be placed in the freezer. The colder, the better.)

To assemble Pour cream into a clean, stainless steel bowl and, using a hand mixer, beat until soft peaks form. Spoon whipped cream over tart and spread evenly on top. Finely grate lime zest over cream and finish with chopped mint, toasted coconut, and crumbled toasted meringue.

Slow-cooked chicken

6 chicken legs, bone-in, skin-on

Salt and freshly ground black pepper

2 Tbsp canola oil

6 Tbsp extra-virgin olive oil

10 tomatillos, husked, washed, and halved

3 poblano chilies, stemmed, seeded, and quartered lengthwise

1 small onion, sliced

4 cloves garlic, crushed

1 tsp fennel seeds

Juice and zest of 2 limes

¼ cup white wine

1 cup chicken stock

½ bunch fresh cilantro, stems and roots chopped (set aside leaves for garnish)

1 Tbsp salt

Corn pudding

8 ears of corn, kernels removed

¼ cup water

½ cup butter, cut into 1-inch pieces

½ Tbsp salt

Assembly

½ cup finely grated Parmigiano-Reggiano

Butter (optional)

½ cup crumbled fresh soft sheep's milk cheese (such as feta)

Cilantro leaves

½ charred lemon (optional)

Pickled red onion, thinly sliced (optional)

 Serves 6

Slow-Cooked Chicken with Tomatillos, Poblano Peppers, Sheep's Milk Cheese, and Corn Pudding

Slow-cooked chicken Season chicken legs with salt and pepper. Heat canola oil in a frying pan on high. Add chicken legs, skin-side down, and sear for 5 minutes, until golden brown. Flip and sear for another 2 to 3 minutes. Transfer chicken to a plate and set aside.

Heat olive oil in a large heavy-bottomed saucepan on medium-high heat. Add tomatillos and cook for 15 minutes, until browned, blistered, and the juices are released. Add chilies, onions, garlic, fennel seeds, lime juice and zest, and wine and cook for 5 minutes, until wine has reduced by a quarter.

Add chicken to the pan, pour in stock, and add cilantro stems and roots and salt. Ensure that three-quarters of the chicken is covered in liquid (add more stock, if needed). Cover, reduce heat to low, and simmer for 30 minutes. Stir gently, cover, and cook for another 45 to 60 minutes, until the meat falls off the bone. The end result should be slightly soupy. If there is too much liquid and you want to thicken and intensify the stock,

carefully transfer the chicken to a plate, increase heat to high, and boil, uncovered, for 5 minutes, or until the sauce has thickened. Return chicken to the pan.

Corn pudding Preheat the oven to 300°F. Place corn kernels and water into a blender, working in batches if necessary, and purée for several minutes, until silky smooth. Transfer corn to a small roasting pan, add butter and salt, stir, and bake for about 30 minutes. Stir and then bake for another 60 minutes, until thickened. (You want the pudding to cook down very slowly to reduce and concentrate its naturally sweet flavour.)

To assemble Stir Parmigiano-Reggiano into the corn pudding and add a knob of butter, if desired.

Spoon a generous amount of corn pudding into a wide-rimmed plate or wide bowl and spread it out slightly, leaving a well in the centre. Spoon a chicken leg and a generous amount of sauce into the well. Garnish with sheep's milk cheese and cilantro leaves, plus lemon and red onion, if using.

The Gabardine

Graham Pratt

Graham!!

A MUCH-NEEDED GASTROPUB outpost brightens a grey banker's stretch of Bay Street. The food may be hardy, but the room is Parisian pretty with whitewashed brick walls and an elbow-to-elbow marble bar that encourages mingling—and food envy. At the heart of that envy is chef Graham Pratt's generous cooking, full of comfort and craft (including craft beer). Mac 'n' cheese, chicken pot pie, sirloin cheeseburgers, and desserts like pie and ice cream waffle sandwiches are the type of food you want in your life. Pratt veers to other countries too, taking inspiration from places like Lisbon, where he recently tried *açorda de bacalhau* for the first time. "The server explained to me that it was something your grandma would cook for you, and that is always a good thing," says Pratt of experiencing the instant appeal of Portuguese comfort food. He's also an avid smoker of meat, even doing pop-ups under the moniker Simcoe Smoke Northern BBQ. "I wanted it to be a Canadian take on southern techniques," he explains. And his recipe for smoked beer can chicken with "chalet" sauce is about as deliciously Canadian as it comes.

2 lbs salt cod

4 fresh bay leaves

8 cups cold water

2 Tbsp unsalted butter

¼ cup Portuguese olive oil

1 onion, thinly sliced into rings

2 cloves garlic, chopped

2 tsp salt

1 tsp freshly ground black pepper

2 tsp hot chili paste, such as Ferma
Hot Pimento Paste

1 tomato, deseeded and finely
chopped

3 cups day-old crusty bread
(preferably from a Portuguese
bakery), torn into pieces

½ bunch cilantro, roughly
chopped, divided

¼ bunch flat-leaf parsley,
roughly chopped, divided

3 green onions, thinly sliced, for
garnish

6 green olives, pitted and sliced

3 egg yolks

 Serves 4

Açorda de Bacalhau

Soak salt cod in water in the fridge for 3 days, changing water 3 to 4 times a day.

Preheat the oven to 350°F. Clean fish, removing any skin and bones, and cut into 1-inch pieces.

In a large pot on medium-high heat, combine salt cod, bay leaves, and cold water and bring to a low boil, skimming off any impurities that rise to the top. Cook for 10 minutes, until tender. Using a slotted spoon, transfer cod to a plate. Reserve 4 cups of cooking liquid. Shred salt cod, leaving some bigger pieces for a bit of texture, and set aside.

In a wide, shallow frying pan (a "rondeau" pot) on medium heat, warm butter and olive oil. Add onions and cook for 5 to 8 minutes, until translucent. Add garlic, salt, and pepper and cook on medium-low heat for 2 minutes, until onions just start to caramelize. Stir in chili paste and tomato. Cover and cook for another 5 minutes, until tomato breaks down.

Add salt cod and cook for 2 to 3 minutes, until softened. Add reserved cod cooking liquid and bread. Cook for another 5 to 10 minutes, stirring often, until bread has absorbed all the liquid and mixture becomes thick and glutinous, like risotto. Add three-quarters of the chopped cilantro and parsley.

Transfer mixture to a baking dish and bake for 5 to 10 minutes, until a crust has formed. Combine remaining herbs, green onions, olives, and egg yolks in a bowl and use as garnish.

Chicken

1½ tsp salt

1 tsp coarsely ground black pepper

1 tsp poultry seasoning

2 Tbsp unsalted butter, melted

1 "roaster" chicken (3½ lbs)

1 (473 ml) can amber lager, divided

½ bag of maple wood chips, soaked in water

Fresh thyme leaves, for garnish

Sauce

2 Tbsp unsalted butter

1 shallot, finely chopped

2 cloves garlic, finely chopped

½ Tbsp chopped fresh thyme leaves

2 tsp poultry seasoning

½ tsp freshly ground black pepper

¼ tsp ground allspice

¼ tsp ground ginger

½ tsp paprika

2 Tbsp all-purpose flour

½ can reserved beer

1 tsp hot sauce, such as Frank's RedHot

½ tsp Worcestershire sauce

1 Tbsp ketchup

1 Tbsp white vinegar

2 cups chicken stock

 Serves 4

Smoked Beer Can Chicken with "Chalet" Sauce

Chicken In a small bowl, combine salt, pepper, poultry seasoning, and butter and generously rub mixture over the whole chicken.

Pour half of the beer into a small bowl and reserve it for the sauce. Place the chicken over the can, cavity-side down, and balance the legs to keep it standing like a tripod.

Start a quarter of a bag of lump hardwood charcoal on one side of a barbecue. Once all the coals are lit, add another couple of handfuls of charcoal and heat to a temperature of between 250°F and 300°F.

Using the beer can as a stand, place chicken on the opposite side of the barbecue from the charcoal. Place a handful of wood chips over the coals, cover, and maintain the temperature by adding charcoal and wood chips periodically.

Cook chicken for 1½ to 2 hours, or until a thermometer registers 160°F to 165°F when inserted into the thickest part of the breast. Reserve the can of beer.

Sauce In a small saucepan on medium-low heat, melt butter. Add shallots, garlic, and thyme, and cook for 2 minutes, until shallots are translucent. Add poultry seasoning and spices and cook for another minute. Add flour, stir to make a roux, and cook for 30 seconds. Slowly whisk in beer, a little at a time, allowing the roux to absorb the liquid before adding more. Add remaining ingredients and the smoky beer from the can used on the barbecue. Cook for another 10 minutes on medium heat, until sauce is glossy and slightly thickened.

To assemble Carve chicken and transfer to a serving platter. Wash and dry beer can and transfer sauce into can. (Alternatively, drink a beer and use a fresh empty.) Sprinkle chicken with fresh thyme, and when ready to serve, pour sauce directly from the can.

The Hearth

Lora Kirk and Lynn Crawford

Lora ADDIE PEPPER *Lynn*

SOMETIMES I ARRIVE EARLY to Pearson airport just so I can sit down at The Hearth and relax over a nice breakfast. (As a naturally late riser, this is significant.) Chefs Lynn Crawford and Lora Kirk will suck you in with their hospitality and soulful cooking, motivating you too to arrive two hours before your scheduled departure time. Some of the fan favourites served at Ruby Watchco, their popular Riverside restaurant, make appearances here, but the stars of the show are The Hearth's own creations: hearty steel-cut oat porridge with apple and cranberry compote, or their Benedict, which has poached eggs and peameal resting on a fresh-baked cheddar biscuit and drizzled with a golden glaze of hollandaise. A healthy lunch could mean butternut squash soup with sweet corn, black beans, and chipotle cream, or an especially proud Canadian moment with fish tacos made with Fogo Island cod. To have this prized, hand-caught fish on any menu in Toronto, let alone an airport menu, is something truly special, made even more so when fried to a crisp and tucked into these delectable tacos. And I'd travel far and wide just to have another slice of their classic carrot cake with cream cheese icing: a taste of home before you roam.

Parmesan garlic bread

½ cup mayonnaise

6 cloves garlic, minced

1 Tbsp Sriracha

2 Tbsp finely chopped chives

½ cup finely grated Parmigiano-Reggiano cheese

1 thin baguette, cut in half lengthwise

Salt and freshly ground black pepper

French onion soup

2 Tbsp extra-virgin olive oil

2 Tbsp unsalted butter

2 cloves garlic, minced

6 large Vidalia onions, halved and cut into ¼-inch slices

3 Tbsp granulated sugar

2 sprigs fresh thyme

1 bay leaf

6 cups hot good-quality beef stock

1 cup dry white wine

¼ cup cognac (optional)

Kosher salt and freshly ground black pepper

1 cup grated Gruyère

 Serves 6

French Onion Soup with Parmesan Garlic Bread

Parmesan garlic bread Preheat the oven to 350°F. Place a rack on the middle shelf.

In a bowl, combine mayonnaise, garlic, Sriracha, chives, and Parmigiano-Reggiano and mix to a smooth paste. Spread mixture evenly on the cut sides of the baguette. Place baguette, face up, on a rimmed baking sheet and bake for 15 minutes, until golden. Slice baguette, diagonally, into ½-inch-thick pieces. Season with salt and pepper.

French onion soup In a large heavy-bottomed stockpot on medium heat, combine olive oil and butter. Add garlic, onions, sugar, thyme, and bay leaf and sauté for 15 minutes, or until onions have started to darken at the edges. Reduce heat to low and cook, uncovered, for 1 hour, until onions are caramelized and the bottom of the pot is covered in a rich, dark, nutty-brown film.

Add stock and wine, increase heat to medium, and simmer for 15 minutes. Stir in cognac (if using) and season with salt and pepper.

Preheat a broiler. Ladle soup into 6 ramekins and top each with 3 Parmesan garlic croutons and a generous handful of Gruyère. Place ramekins on a baking sheet and broil for about 5 minutes, until Gruyère is golden and melted. Serve immediately.

Spicy citrus slaw

½ cup mayonnaise

½ cup sour cream

Juice and zest of 1 lime

Juice and zest of 1 lemon

¾ cup cilantro leaves, divided

1 Tbsp Sriracha

Salt and freshly ground black pepper

¼ large head green cabbage, thinly sliced (about 4 cups)

4 green onions, thinly sliced

Fish taco

1 cup all-purpose flour

1 cup white rice flour

2 tsp kosher salt

2 cups club soda

8 cups vegetable oil, for deep-frying

2 lbs skinless Fogo Island cod fillets

Salt and freshly ground black pepper

16 small flour tortillas

2 avocados, sliced, for garnish

1–2 sprigs cilantro, leaves only, for garnish

2 Tbsp sliced pickled jalapeños, for garnish

1 lime, cut into 8 wedges, for garnish

 Serves 8

Fogo Island Fish Tacos with Spicy Citrus Slaw

Spicy citrus slaw In a blender, combine mayonnaise, sour cream, lime and lemon juice and zest, half of the cilantro leaves, and Sriracha. Blend together and season with salt and pepper. In a large bowl, combine cabbage and green onions, toss, and mix in ¼ cup of dressing to start. Add more to taste. Set aside.

Fish taco Preheat the oven to 350°F. In a medium bowl, combine flours and salt and mix well. Whisk in club soda and stir until smooth, with no lumps. The batter should be just thick enough to coat the fish. (Add a bit more club soda or flour to achieve the desired consistency.)

Heat vegetable oil in a deep fryer or large saucepan on medium-high, until the temperature reaches 350°F. Coat fish in batter, allow the excess to drip off, and carefully lower, in batches of 5 or 6, into oil. Cook fish for 5 minutes, turning occasionally with a slotted spoon and maintaining oil temperature at 350°F, until crust is crisp and golden brown. Using a slotted spoon, transfer fish to a wire rack set on top of a baking sheet. Season with salt and pepper.

Wrap a stack of tortillas in foil and heat in oven until warmed through.

Top each tortilla with fish, slaw, avocado, the remaining cilantro leaves, and pickled jalapeños. Serve with lime wedges.

Honest Weight

Jason Yee and
Kenneth Gilmore

IT WAS BY CHANCE that I met John Bil on Prince Edward Island a decade ago. A friend had invited me along to a so-called kitchen party, which turned out to be a backwoods bash full of beer, music, and fun people. Double-fisting cold brews and singing along to blaring rock, I noted that the oysters I was slurping back in the middle of the woods were the best I'd ever had, anywhere. Now, as I sit down at a polished wood table at Honest Weight in the Junction, it all makes sense. Conceived by John Bil and Victoria Bazan, and backed by a team of talented chefs, including Kenneth Gilmore and Jason Yee, as a breezily charming restaurant and fish shop, it's got a focal-point counter for retail mongering where, on this summer's day, the fish and seafood is pan-Canadian. There are plump mussels from Salt Spring Island, Ontario rainbow trout, and show-stopping Quebec snow crab, to name a few. But do stay to taste the good stuff spun into dishes like okonomiyaki (a Japanese-style fish and seafood pancake)—homey, earthy, delicate, and saucy. The chowder is naturally thick and creamy, and obviously you'll want fresh oysters too. And just like that, I'm back in the woods of Prince Edward Island.

Infused cream
1 Tbsp vegetable oil
2 onions, finely diced
2 cloves garlic, minced
1 small fennel bulb, finely diced
4 ribs celery, finely diced
1 tsp whole black peppercorns
2 bay leaves
1 tsp fennel seeds
4 sprigs fresh thyme
1 cup dry white wine
4¼ cups whipping (35%) cream

Potato
1 lb Yukon Gold potatoes

Shellfish
2 lbs mussels (Salt Spring
   Island, PEI, or Newfoundland),
   cleaned
2 lbs clams (Savoury, Manila,
   or Littleneck), cleaned

Assembly
Salt and freshly ground
   black pepper
Finely chopped chives,
   for garnish

 Serves 4–6

Honest Weight Chowder

Infused cream Heat vegetable oil in a medium saucepan on medium. Add onions, garlic, fennel, and celery and cook for 10 minutes, until translucent. Place peppercorns, bay leaves, fennel seeds, and thyme in a 10-inch square cheesecloth. Bring the corners of the cheesecloth together and tie with a length of kitchen string to form a pouch. Add the pouch to the saucepan. Add wine, bring to a boil, and cook until reduced by half. Reduce heat to low, stir in cream, and simmer for 30 minutes. Discard the pouch. Cover infused cream and set aside.

Potato Bring a pot of salted water to a boil on high heat, add potatoes, and cook for 15 minutes, until tender. Drain, allow potatoes to cool, and cut into ¼-inch cubes. Set aside.

Shellfish Place mussels and clams in a large pot with 1 inch of water. Bring to a boil on high heat, and cook for 3 to 5 minutes, until mussels and clams open. Discard any unopened mussels or clams. Set aside to cool. Pick out mussel and clam meat and set aside. Discard shells. Strain remaining cooking liquid through a fine-mesh sieve and reserve.

To assemble Add reserved cooking liquid, mussel and clam meat, and potatoes to the saucepan with the infused cream and warm on medium heat. Season to taste with salt and pepper. Garnish with chives. Serve hot.

Batter

2 cups all-purpose flour

2 tsp dashi powder

4 Tbsp peeled and grated Chinese yam (Shan Yao)

2 eggs

2 cups water

4 Tbsp soy sauce

Pancake

4 tsp vegetable oil, divided

2 cups mixed seafood (shrimp, squid, salmon, cod), cut into bite-size pieces

6 cups shredded cabbage

4 eggs

12 thin slices of bacon, cut into 5-inch lengths

Okonomi sauce, to drizzle

Kewpie mayonnaise, to drizzle

Bonito flakes, for garnish

4 Tbsp finely sliced green onions, for garnish

 **Makes 4 pancakes**

Okonomiyaki

Batter In a mixing bowl, sift flour and dashi powder. Add yam and eggs, then water and soy sauce and mix until smooth, with the consistency of pancake batter. Add more water if batter is too thick. Refrigerate for 1 hour.

Pancake Heat 1 tsp vegetable oil in a non-stick pan on medium. Pour a ladle of pancake batter into the pan and tilt the pan to spread batter out into a 6-inch circle. Spread ½ cup of mixed seafood on top of the batter, followed by a quarter of the shredded cabbage. Make a well in the middle of the cabbage and crack in an egg. Top with 3 slices of bacon, side by side, and cook for 3 to 5 minutes.

Using a wide spatula, carefully flip pancake over, bacon-side down, and gather any cabbage or garnishes to form a circle. Cook for 5 to 7 minutes, until seafood is cooked through and pancake is nicely browned.

Transfer to a plate with the bacon facing up. Apply a thin drizzle of okonomi sauce and mayonnaise to the entire pancake. Sprinkle generously with bonito flakes and green onions. Repeat for remaining 3 pancakes. Serve immediately.

Indian Street Food Co.

Hemant Bhagwani

AN INNOVATOR IN THIS CITY'S restaurant scene, Hemant Bhagwani does things differently, as evidenced by his Amaya group of restaurants and quick-service Amaya Express spots. His was one of the first Indian restaurants to do wine pairings, and one of the first in Toronto to implement a no-tipping policy. Even at Amaya Express, half a dozen men and women are chopping peppers and wok-cooking silky sauces. One is slapping naan dough before smacking it onto the inside of the tandoor oven—the bread is made to order (at a food court, no less). Like most people who push boundaries, Bhagwani clearly didn't get the memo, and Indian Street Food Co. is a more wonderful restaurant because of it. Many dishes, such as the popular cauliflower or chili crab, are designed as a nod to the disappearing street hawkers of Delhi and Mumbai. The corn pakoras with spinach curry are a play on his mom's malai corn back home; and the wondrous chaat is a textural and taste sensation of puffed rice, pomegranate, potato, tamarind chutney, chickpeas, and yogurt.

Corn pakoras

½ cup corn kernels

2 Tbsp vegetable oil

1 tsp chopped fresh ginger

1 tsp chopped garlic

1 tsp finely chopped
green bird's-eye chili

5 Tbsp canned creamed
corn

2 Tbsp coconut milk

½ tsp garam masala

Salt

6 Tbsp whole milk

2 tsp cornstarch

1 tsp chopped cilantro
leaves

1 tsp chopped green
onions

½ cup polenta

Spinach curry

3 cups baby spinach leaves

4 tsp ghee or clarified butter

1 bay leaf

2 mild red chilies

4 tsp chopped onion

1 tsp chopped fresh ginger

1 tsp chopped garlic

1 tsp green chili pepper

1 tsp ground coriander

1 tsp ground cumin

1 tsp Kashmiri red chili
powder

½ tsp garam masala

2 Tbsp chopped tomato

4 tsp unsalted butter

2 tsp chopped cilantro
leaves

Poppadoms, cut in small
pieces and fried until
golden, for garnish

 Serves 2

Creamy Spinach Curry with Grilled Polenta-Crusted Corn Pakoras

Corn pakoras Place corn kernels in a blender and purée to a paste.

Heat vegetable oil in a frying pan on high. Add ginger, garlic, and chili and sauté 1 to 2 minutes, until fragrant. Add corn paste and creamed corn and stir. Add coconut milk, garam masala, and salt to taste and simmer for 2 minutes. Add milk, and when it starts to boil, reduce heat to medium-low and add cornstarch. Whisking continuously so that lumps do not form, cook for 30 seconds, or until mixture has thickened. Finish with chopped cilantro and green onions.

Pour prepared mixture onto a small rimmed baking tray, spread evenly, and refrigerate for at least 4 hours, until mixture has set. Using a 1-inch round cookie cutter, cut into pakoras. Dust each side with polenta.

Warm a griddle to medium-high heat. Grill pakoras for 2 to 3 minutes, until golden and crisp.

Spinach curry Bring a pot of salted water to a boil, add spinach leaves, and blanch for 1 minute. Drain and transfer spinach to a bowl of ice water. Squeeze out excess water, place in a blender, and purée.

Heat ghee or clarified butter in a frying pan on high. Add bay leaf and whole red chilies and sauté for 1 minute. Add onions, ginger, garlic, and green chili and sauté for another 1 to 2 minutes. Add coriander, cumin, red chili powder, and garam masala and sauté for another minute. Add tomatoes and cook well. (Add some water if mixture appears too dry.) Add spinach purée and cook for another 8 minutes. Finish with butter and chopped cilantro leaves.

To assemble Place spinach curry in a bowl and top with corn pakoras. Garnish with poppadoms and serve immediately.

¼ cup unsalted butter

3 Tbsp vegetable oil

8–10 cloves garlic, chopped

20 whole black peppercorns, crushed in a pestle and mortar

2-inch piece fresh ginger, chopped

6–8 green onions, roughly chopped

1 Dungeness crab, cleaned and legs and claws removed (or 11 oz fresh crabmeat)

1 tsp chopped green bird's-eye chili

2 Tbsp chopped fresh dill

2 Tbsp chopped cilantro, including stems

Salt

1 lime

Malabar paratha or soft pau (burger buns), to serve (optional)

 Serves 2

Mumbai Chili Crab

Heat butter and vegetable oil in a heavy-bottomed pan on medium-high. Add garlic and sauté for 1 to 2 minutes, until golden brown. Add crushed peppercorns, ginger, and green onions and sauté gently for another minute. Add the crab legs and carapace to the pan and cook for 12 minutes (if using crabmeat, sauté for 2 to 3 minutes), adding a little water if the crab begins to stick to the pan. Stir in chili, dill, and cilantro and cook for another 2 minutes. Season with salt and finish with a squeeze of lime.

Assemble the crab legs and claws on a platter, then spoon the chili crab mixture over top. Garnish with edible flowers, if desired, and serve with any extra sauce and malabar paratha or soft pau, if using.

Kinka
Izakaya

Ippei Iwata

IF YOU'RE NOT easily frightened by shouted greetings and goodbyes, have I got the place for you! A restaurant that has you drinking sake out of a large bamboo vessel is a restaurant that wants you to have fun. So loosen your tie and enjoy the ride. With locations in Toronto, Montreal, and Japan, this spirited Japanese izakaya (small plates) joint is as fun to be in as it is to eat in. Sweet and salty pork belly is served in its luscious braising liquid, while the agedashi tofu—the ultimate soft tofu dish—is as soothing as a Sunday morning. The Bloor Street location feels like a slice of side-street Tokyo, with square wooden stools and shared tables. For an even more authentic experience, slide off your shoes, slide into some slippers, and take a step up to the dining area, featuring squat Japanese chabudai tables and pillows for sitting. Menu items and specials are endlessly appealing, from Atlantic lobster sashimi and Kinoko bibimbap—in which rice, mushrooms, and Gruyère are tossed together in a sizzling stone bowl—to a carbonara udon, silky salmon *tataki*, and good old *karaage* (marinated fried chicken with garlic mayo). Amidst the kind, swift service, there's happy yelling, drinking, and lots of good times.

1½ cups vegetable oil

1 pork belly (2¾ lbs), cut into 2½-inch cubes

1 cup brown cane sugar

1¼ cups soy sauce

2 cloves garlic, crushed

2-inch piece fresh ginger, unpeeled and cut in half

10 cups water

 Serves 5

Kakuni (Japanese Braised Pork Belly)

Heat vegetable oil in a saucepan on medium-high until it reaches 350°F. (Alternatively, use a deep fryer). Working in batches if necessary, gently lower in pork belly and deep-fry, undisturbed, for 5 minutes, until golden brown. Using a slotted spoon, transfer pork belly to a plate lined with paper towels.

In a large pot, combine pork belly, brown cane sugar, soy sauce, garlic, and ginger and add enough water to cover. Bring to a boil on high heat, then reduce heat to medium and simmer for 2 hours, covered, until pork belly is tender. Serve pork belly with some braising liquid.

¾ cup mirin
¼ cup + 2 Tbsp sake
¼ cup + 2 Tbsp soy sauce
1½ cups water
4 tsp liquid seaweed dashi
1½ cups vegetable oil
Potato starch, for coating
2 packages (10½ oz each) soft
    tofu, cut into 1-inch cubes

6 Tbsp grated daikon,
    for garnish
2 Tbsp grated fresh ginger,
    for garnish
2 green onions, finely
    chopped, for garnish
2 Tbsp chopped nori,
    for garnish

 Serves 6

Agedashi Tofu

In a small saucepan on medium heat, bring mirin and sake to a boil. Add soy sauce, water, and dashi, stir, and return to a boil. Reduce heat to low and cover (to prevent evaporation) to keep warm.

Heat vegetable oil in a saucepan on medium-high until it reaches 350°F. (Alternatively, use a deep fryer.) Place potato starch on a shallow plate and gently roll tofu pieces in the starch, until evenly coated on each side. Dust off excess starch, gently lower tofu into vegetable oil, and deep-fry for 8 minutes, until tofu has puffed up and started to float, and its sides are crispy. Using a slotted spoon, transfer tofu to a wire rack and let drain.

To serve, pour dashi into six deep serving dishes. Carefully lower fried tofu into each. Garnish with daikon, ginger, green onions, and nori.

Leña Restaurante

Julie Marteleira and
Anthony Walsh

THE BUZZ WAS BUILDING long before the glass doors swung open for the newest Oliver & Bonacini offering. And for corporate executive chef Anthony Walsh, Leña is the most personal of the restaurant group's locations, as it's grounded in Latin cuisine and pays homage to his Argentinean mother-in-law, Elena. With executive chef Julie Marteleira showcasing her own Portuguese heritage with shining dishes such as the cloud of a dessert that is her egg-white flan, this breakfast-to-dinner restaurant is composed of three large rooms decked out to impress—part ode to the old Hudson's Bay building's art deco past on the main floor, part moody scene-stealer down below, and all handshakes and lemony saffron-braised

chicken up above. If the three-martini lunch ever makes a comeback, this is where it will happen. But getting back to Walsh . . . A mentor to many chefs in the industry, he's composed a menu full of substance and heart. Breakfast's savoury palmito buns and dulce de leche yogurt parfaits move to cocktail hour's snacky mini beef empanadas and smoked jamón croquettes, and on to dinner's saucy rabbit with snails, pretty crudos, steamed clams, fresh salads, churros, and chocolate. It's a deep and delicious exploration of a remarkable cuisine that is relatively new to this city. Now go kiss your mother-in-law.

Slow-cooked salmon

2 Tbsp kosher salt

3 Tbsp granulated sugar

Zest of 1 lemon

1 tsp fennel seeds, toasted

1 tsp coriander seeds, toasted

1 tsp white peppercorn, toasted

1 tsp coarsely ground dried chili

4 boneless, skinless wild salmon fillets (about 3 oz each), centre-cut

¼ cup canola or grapeseed oil

1 small fennel bulb, cut into ⅛-inch-thick slices

1 bunch green onions, cut in half lengthwise and greens cut into 1-inch batons

½ cup radishes (such as breakfast, Misato Rose, or Valentine), cut into ⅛-inch-thick slices

Salad and dressing

½ cup Jerusalem artichokes, well-scrubbed and cut into ⅛-inch slices

2 tsp fresh lemon juice

¼ cup extra-virgin olive oil, plus extra for drizzling

1½ Tbsp fresh lemon juice

½ tsp Dijon mustard (or your favourite hot mustard)

Salt and freshly ground black pepper

½ cup chopped fresh herbs (e.g., mint, dill, flat-leaf parsley, and tarragon)

 Serves 4

Slow-Cooked Salmon with Wilted Onions, Fennel, and Jerusalem Artichokes

Slow-cooked salmon Using a mortar and pestle or food processor, combine salt, sugar, lemon zest, and spices. Grind or pulse until well combined. Generously season salmon with mixture and set aside for 2 to 3 hours at room temperature.

Dip salmon into a bowl of cold water (don't agitate it too much) and pat dry with paper towels. Place fillets in a resealable plastic bag with canola or grapeseed oil and refrigerate for 2 to 3 hours.

Remove fillets from bag and wipe gently. (They don't have to be completely dry.) Set aside at room temperature for 30 minutes.

Preheat the oven to 325°F. Spread sliced fennel and green onions on a rimmed baking sheet. Bake the vegetables for 5 to 6 minutes. Reduce heat to 275°F. Place salmon fillets on top, flesh-side up, and bake for 7 to 10 minutes. Rotate the baking sheet 180 degrees and bake for another 5 to 6 minutes. Transfer salmon to a warm plate and set aside while you assemble the salad.

Salad and dressing In a small bowl, combine Jerusalem artichokes and lemon juice. Mix and set aside. Place wilted fennel and green onions into another bowl, add radishes and artichokes, and mix well.

For the dressing, combine olive oil, lemon juice, and mustard in a small mixing bowl. Whisk and season lightly to taste. Add herbs and mix gently. Pour dressing over salad and toss to combine.

To assemble Divide salad between 4 plates, top with salmon, and finish with freshly ground black pepper and a drizzle of olive oil. Serve immediately.

2–3 lbs fresh rabbit, separated into fore quarter, hind quarter, and saddle

Kosher salt and freshly ground black pepper

2 Tbsp extra-virgin olive oil, plus extra for frying

1 Tbsp toasted fennel seeds, lightly crushed

1 tsp chili flakes

1 fennel bulb, diced and fronds reserved

1 Spanish onion, diced

4 cloves garlic, chopped

1 rib celery, diced

4 bay leaves

⅓ cup honey

1 cup mixed olives

¾ cup sherry vinegar

1 Tbsp sweet paprika

1 Tbsp good-quality dried oregano

2 cups good-quality chicken stock

3 cups tomato passata, or good-quality crushed strained tomatoes

Fresh noodles or cooked polenta, to serve

 Serves 6–8

Rabbit with Olives, Honey, and Vinegar

Generously season rabbit with salt and pepper. Heat 2 Tbsp olive oil in a large casserole dish on medium. Add rabbit, skin-side down, and sear for 5 to 7 minutes, or until golden brown. Flip and sear for another 5 to 7 minutes. (Work in batches to avoid overcrowding, if necessary.) Transfer rabbit to a plate and set aside.

Place the casserole dish back on the stovetop, reduce heat to medium-low, and add fennel seeds and chili flakes. Cook for 1 minute, until fragrant. Add fennel, onions, garlic, celery, and bay leaves, and cook for another 3 minutes. (Add a little more olive oil, if necessary, to help the browning.) Add honey, increase heat to medium-high, and cook for another 2 to 3 minutes. (You'll smell the caramel as the honey reduces.) Add olives, stir, and cook for another 2 to 3 minutes. Add vinegar, paprika, and oregano and cook for another minute.

Return rabbit to the dish, add chicken stock and passata, and bring to a simmer on medium-low heat. Cook, partially covered, for another 1½ hours. If the ragu looks too soupy, remove the lid and cook until you have the desired consistency. If it's too dry, add an extra splash of broth, cover, and simmer away. Season with salt and pepper.

Chop reserved fennel fronds and use to finish the rabbit. Serve with fresh noodles or polenta.

Live Organic
Food Bar
Jennifer Italiano

JENNIFER ITALIANO AND her co-owner brother Christopher Italiano's groundbreaking hub for plant-based food is colourful and streamlined, yet homey too. Generous organic, vegan, and gluten- and wheat-free meals are served without guilt but with loads of quotation marks: there are the crave-worthy nachos with corn chips, sunflower "refried beans," guacamole, salsa, walnut "taco meat," cashew "sour cream," and cashew cheese. Some of the most popular items include imaginative twists on go-to classics, such as Jennifer's pulled burdock burrito and the vegan manicotti. "The pretty and satisfying zucchini manicotti with cashew dill ricotta is a Live staple," she says. She suggests preparing the main ingredients a day ahead, making for quick and impressive assembly around dinnertime. Meanwhile, her "cheesecake" with local strawberry sauce is a no-bake delight and the perfect capper at your next dinner party. "Your guests won't even know it's vegan," she promises. Delicious food (and amazing juices and smoothies) that makes you feel better for eating it? That's just one of many reasons why this healthy spot is still so hot.

Crust
6–8 Medjool dates
2½ cups shelled walnuts
¼ tsp grey salt

Filling
1 vanilla bean
2½ cups raw cashews, covered
  in warm water and soaked
  overnight
¾ cup coconut milk
¾ cup agave syrup
⅓ tsp grey salt
¾ cup water, room temperature
¾ cup coconut oil, room
  temperature

Strawberry sauce
1 cup fresh strawberries,
  trimmed
1 Tbsp agave syrup
1 Tbsp fresh lemon juice

 Serves 8–12

"Cheesecake" with Strawberry Sauce

Crust Place dates in a bowl, fill with warm water, and soak for 4 to 6 hours. Drain and set aside.

Line a 9-inch round cake pan with parchment paper or plastic wrap and set aside. (Alternatively, use a springform pan, but cover the bottom with plastic wrap to prevent sticking.)

Place all ingredients in a food processor and pulse until finely chopped. Do not overmix. Pour mixture into the lined pan and spread evenly. (You may need to use a little water to help spread the crust.) Press firmly into the pan.

Filling Split vanilla bean lengthwise and scrape out seeds into a high-speed blender or food processor. Drain cashews, rinse, and add to the blender. Add coconut milk, agave syrup, salt, and water and blend. Gradually add coconut oil, scraping the sides of the blender as needed to ensure all ingredients are incorporated and smooth. Scrape filling into the pan and smooth the surface. Freeze for at least 3 hours or overnight until ready to serve.

Strawberry sauce Place all ingredients in a blender or food processor and purée until smooth.

To assemble About an hour before serving, remove cheesecake from freezer. Gently run a knife around the edge of the pan and release cake from the pan. Cut into wedges, place each slice onto a plate, and drizzle with strawberry sauce. Leftover cheesecake can be stored in the fridge for a couple of days or refrozen.

Cashew-dill ricotta

1½ cups raw cashews, covered in
hot water and soaked overnight
3 Tbsp chopped fresh dill
2 Tbsp finely chopped onion
2 cloves garlic
2 Tbsp nutritional yeast
2 Tbsp fresh lemon juice
¾ tsp grey salt
Water, to thin mixture (optional)

Red pepper marinara

1 clove garlic
1–2 tsp fresh lemon juice
½ tsp grey salt
½ tsp cayenne
¼ cup sun-dried tomatoes,
covered in warm water and
soaked for 4–6 hours
2 field tomatoes, diced
1 red pepper, seeded
2 Tbsp extra-virgin olive oil

Hemp seed basil pesto

1 cup fresh basil leaves
3 Tbsp raw hemp seeds
1 clove garlic
1 tsp fresh lemon juice
Salt and freshly ground black
pepper
¼ cup cold-pressed olive oil,
plus extra if needed

Assembly

2–3 zucchini, ends trimmed
1 cup sprouts or microgreens,
to serve
Fresh dill, to serve

 Serves 4

Zucchini Manicotti with Cashew-Dill Ricotta

Cashew-dill ricotta Drain cashews and set aside. In a food processor, combine dill, onions, garlic, yeast, lemon juice, and salt and pulse until a paste is formed. Add cashews and mix until very smooth yet fairly firm. Add a little water to loosen mixture up, if necessary.

Red pepper marinara In a food processor, combine garlic, lemon juice, salt, and cayenne and pulse.

Drain sun-dried tomatoes and add to mixture, along with tomatoes, red pepper, and olive oil and process until smooth.

Hemp seed basil pesto Place basil, hemp seeds, and garlic in a food processor and pulse until finely chopped, scraping down sides as needed. Add lemon juice, and salt and pepper to taste. Gradually drizzle in olive oil until mixed. If pesto is too thick to dollop, thin out with additional oil.

To assemble Using a mandolin, cut zucchini lengthwise into very thin slices. You will need 32 slices in total (8 per person). Lay slices on a cutting board. Spoon 1 heaping tsp of cashew-dill ricotta on top and spread along the surface. Roll to enclose the filling.

To serve, spread ¼ cup of pesto around the perimeter of each of 4 plates, then place 8 zucchini rolls horizontally across the plate. You can stack some or leave them neatly beside each other, depending on how creative you feel. Dollop some marinara on the rolls and top with more pesto. Garnish with sprouts or microgreens and a few sprigs of dill. Serve at room temperature.

Loka
Dave Mottershall

TORONTO'S FIRST KICKSTARTER-FUNDED restaurant is the heart and soul of chef Dave Mottershall, who launched this personal exploration of Canadian cuisine after making a name for himself with farmers and foragers through his pop-ups around town. And by cooking professionally for 20 years, from Banff to PEI, he's become known as a chef who would accept a handful of ingredients—be they berries or bison—perhaps dehydrate them, and turn them into a syrup, a powder, or a pickle. Mottershall is about great taste and zero waste. As well, there's a focus on whole butchery within this Queen West restaurant, and the house-cured charcuterie is the lucky offshoot, including pig heart nduja (a spreadable salami from Calabria, here served with smoked goat yogurt and burnt honey) and a supple duck breast prosciutto, dry-cured for six months. Pan-roasted mushrooms with truffled potatoes and deer lichen is as accessible as it is original. So, too, pickled Arctic char with watermelon remoulade and crispy leeks. "We received sagamite [white corn] and haskap from Quebec and were inspired by the classic Quebecois *pouding chomeur* [a baked maple pudding popular during sugar-shack season] to create a recipe that used unfamiliar ingredients in a familiar way," he explains of the featured dessert. The curiosity and thoughtfulness shine through. And it's not just about using different ingredients for the sake of being different. When you put it all together, it makes delicious sense.

1 tsp canola oil

1 clove garlic, minced

1 shallot, minced

3 sprigs fresh thyme

1 lb mussels, cleaned

1 cup white wine

¼ lb pancetta, finely diced

4 ribs celery, finely diced

3 large carrots, finely diced

2 onions, finely diced

4 large potatoes, diced

2 cups unsalted butter

2 cups all-purpose flour

8½ cups whole milk

4¼ cups whipping (35%) cream

1 lb haddock, cut into 1-inch pieces (about 3 cups)

Salt and freshly ground black pepper

3 Tbsp chopped chives, for garnish

Serves 8–12

East Coast Mussel Haddock Chowder

In a large saucepan on medium heat, warm canola oil. Sauté garlic, shallots, and thyme for 1 minute. Add mussels and stir. Add wine and cook for 5 to 7 minutes, until mussels open. Strain mussels, reserving stock. Discard any mussels that didn't open. Remove mussels from the shell and refrigerate for 10 minutes, or until chilled.

In a very large heavy-bottomed pot on medium heat, cook pancetta to release the fat. Add celery, carrots, and onions and sauté for 3 to 5 minutes. Add potatoes and cook for another 3 minutes. Add butter and stir until melted. Stir in flour and cook for 3 to 5 minutes, until nutty and golden.

Add mussel broth to the pot and whisk until smooth. Add milk and cream and continue to whisk. Reduce heat to low and cook, stirring occasionally, for 30 minutes, until vegetables are cooked through. When chowder has thickened, add mussels and haddock and cook for another 10 to 12 minutes, until fish is cooked through and mussels are warm. Season to taste and finish with chopped chives.

Haskap jam

4 cups haskap berries and residual juice

⅓ cup + 2 Tbsp water

2 cups granulated sugar

2 cups water

1 vanilla bean, halved lengthwise and seeds scraped

Vanilla goat yogurt

2 cups goat yogurt

⅓ cup + 2 Tbsp whipping (35%) cream

¼ cup icing sugar

1 Tbsp vanilla extract

Sagamite pudding

2 cups whipping (35%) cream

2 cups best-quality maple syrup

¾ cup unsalted butter, room temperature

1 cup granulated white sugar

2 eggs

1 cup sagamite (coarsely ground white corn)

¾ cup all-purpose flour

1 tsp baking powder

Pinch of salt

Butter, for greasing

 Makes 6 ramekins or 1 (9 × 13-inch) pan

Maple Sagamite with Vanilla Goat Yogurt and Haskap Jam

Haskap jam In a large saucepan on medium-high heat, combine all ingredients and bring to a boil. Cook for 15 to 20 minutes, until reduced by half and jammy.

Vanilla goat yogurt In a large bowl, combine all ingredients and mix well until smooth.

Sagamite pudding Preheat the oven to 400°F.

In a medium saucepan on high heat, combine cream and maple syrup and bring to a boil. Set aside.

Place butter in the bowl of a stand mixer fitted with a paddle attachment and mix at medium speed for 1 minute, until creamy. Add sugar and beat for another minute, until smooth. Add eggs, one at a time, until well incorporated.

In a separate bowl, combine sagamite, flour, baking powder, and salt. Add to the bowl of the stand mixer and mix for 1 minute, until a soft dough forms. Divide dough into greased ramekins or baking dish. Divide cream among the ramekins or spread evenly on top of baking dish. Place on a baking sheet and bake for 12 to 14 minutes (add 15 to 20 minutes extra time if baking in a pan), until a toothpick comes out clean when inserted into the centre.

Serve with whipped goat yogurt and haskap jam or your favourite preserve. Garnish with crumbled toasted hazelnuts and spearmint leaves, if desired.

Maker Pizza

Shlomo Buchler

IT MAY BE tucked off of the Queen West strip, but there's no way you'll miss Maker Pizza—the screamingly yellow and black signage directs you right into the buzzy spot. Then again, why not save yourself the trip altogether and order in? "The delivery market was lacking in quality pizza," says owner Shlomo Buchler. "People have more sophisticated palates than ever and they want better pizza." He hired chef Matty Matheson (VICE TV host and executive chef at Parts & Labour and P&L Catering) to create a menu of craveable pizzas, salads, and sandwiches, and Matheson did just that. The bestselling Frank's Best has goat cheese, frizzled rosemary, roasted garlic, a drizzle of honey, and a sesame crust that tastes like a Montreal bagel. The Apocalypse Cow—with its cheesy, saucy base loaded with mini meatballs and sliced pepperoncini—is a meat-lover's dream. There are even secret-menu pies like the saucy burger-esque Return of the Mac. These offerings are also unique in that the dough is made from "00" flour (unheard of in the delivery market) and the pizza crust is double-baked. "Our pizza is pure Toronto," says Buchler. As for the sandwiches, such as the amazing Eggplant Parm, "Matty had all of these ideas before we opened. When you hear about them they sound fantastic, but when you taste them, they're even better."

3 Tbsp extra-virgin olive oil, divided, plus extra for brushing

½ large white onion, sliced

Salt

2 cups all-purpose flour

4 eggs, beaten

2 cups breadcrumbs

2 eggplant, cut into 1¼-inch-thick slices

1 cup Tomato Sauce (see page 135)

1½ Tbsp grated Parmigiano-Reggiano

16 slices mozzarella

8 roasted jalapeños

½ cup caramelized onions

3–4 strips Roasted Red Peppers (see page 135)

4 Kaiser rolls, halved lengthwise

 Serves 4

Eggplant Parmesan Sandwich

Heat 1 Tbsp olive oil in a large frying pan on low. Add onions and a pinch of salt and cook for 15 to 20 minutes, stirring occasionally, until caramelized. Set aside.

Preheat the oven to 350°F. Using 3 separate shallow bowls, set out flour, eggs, and bread-crumbs. Dip a slice of eggplant into the flour, then the egg, and then the breadcrumbs. Repeat with remaining slices of eggplant.

Heat remaining olive oil in a frying pan on medium. Working in batches to avoid crowding, add eggplant and fry for 2 to 4 minutes, until golden. Flip over and cook for another 2 to 4 minutes, until golden and cooked through.

To build eggplant stacks for your sandwich, ladle ½ cup of tomato sauce into an 8 × 8-inch baking pan and spread evenly. Lay 4 eggplant slices over the sauce. Add more sauce, some Parmigiano-Reggiano, and 1 slice of mozza-rella over each eggplant. Repeat twice. Divide jalapeños, onions, roasted red peppers, and remaining mozzarella slices among eggplant stacks and smother with remaining sauce. Bake for 13 minutes.

Toast Kaiser rolls for 45 seconds in the oven, and then brush with olive oil on both cut sides. Place one eggplant stack on each bun and finish with Parmigiano-Reggiano. Serve immediately.

Tomato sauce

2 cans (28 oz) San Marzano tomatoes

1 can (5½ oz) tomato paste

3 Tbsp extra-virgin olive oil

1 small clove garlic, finely chopped

2 tsp salt

Handful of basil leaves

Meatballs

1¼ lbs ground beef brisket

1¼ lbs ground beef chuck

1 egg

¼ cup grated Parmigiano-Reggiano

¼ cup breadcrumbs

1 Tbsp dried chili flakes

1 Tbsp salt

2 tsp dried oregano

2 tsp dried basil

1½ tsp freshly ground black pepper

¼ cup garlic purée

Roasted red peppers

4 red peppers

Assembly

1 ball pre-made pizza dough

Extra-virgin olive oil, for brushing

1½ Tbsp sesame seeds

½ cup Tomato Sauce (see here)

1 Tbsp grated Parmigiano-Reggiano

2½ cups grated mozzarella

5 pickled pepperoncini, sliced

8–10 strips Roasted Red Peppers (see here)

½ small red onion, thinly sliced

12–15 Meatballs (see here)

10½-oz ball fior di latte, cut into 10–14 cubes

Basil leaves (optional)

 Leftover sauce, meatballs, and peppers can be covered and stored in the refrigerator for several days.

 Serves 2–3

Apocalypse Cow Pizza

Tomato sauce In a large saucepan on high heat, combine all ingredients, blend well with a hand mixer, and bring to a boil. (Alternatively, combine all ingredients in a blender first.) Reduce heat to low and simmer for 1 hour.

Meatballs Preheat the oven to 400°F. In a large bowl, combine all ingredients and mix well. Scoop about a tablespoon of mixture into your hands, form a ball, and place on a baking sheet. Repeat with remaining mixture. Bake for 10 minutes, flip meatballs, and cook for another 5 minutes, until cooked through.

Roasted red peppers Using tongs, hold 1 pepper directly over an open flame until blackened. Repeat with remaining peppers. (Alternatively, preheat a grill or broiler and char peppers for 25 to 35 minutes, or until almost black.) Place peppers in a bowl and cover tightly with plastic wrap. Let sit for 10 minutes, then peel, seed, and slice into strips. Set aside.

To assemble Preheat the oven to 450°F. Stretch pizza dough out into a 16-inch circle and place on a baking sheet. Brush olive oil along the edge of the dough, in a strip about an inch wide, and sprinkle sesame seeds along this edge (they'll stick to the oil). Ladle tomato sauce onto the dough, using the back of the ladle to spread it out. Sprinkle cheeses overtop, and add pepperoncini, red peppers, red onions, and meatballs. Top with fior di latte and bake for 18 to 20 minutes. Serve immediately, topped with basil leaves if using.

Miku
Kazuki
Uchigoshi

BIG IN JAPAN, this new-wave Aburi sushi chain arrived on Toronto's shores in 2016. Aburi-style sushi is sushi-grade fish that's been lightly torched and then, here, topped or sauced with a French spin. With Sapporos in hand (there's also an extensive list of sake, wine, and original cocktails, like the shiso mojito), we mull our options, trying to choose between a host of creative Japanese takes from chef de cuisine Michael Acero and head sushi chef Kazuki Uchigoshi. Aburi beef carpaccio with shoyu egg, Asian pear, edible flowers, wasabi crème fraîche, and jalapeño ponzu? Hai! Ebi fritters? A thousand times, yes! The salmon oshi sushi is smoky, creamy, and smooth, with subtle spicing. Miku's Aburi sockeye

salmon sashimi with Dungeness crab tartare sees seared salmon wrapped around a Dungeness crab tartare filling and garnished with a wasabi–English pea purée. As partners with the Ocean Wise™ conservation program for sustainable seafood, Miku uses wild B.C. sockeye salmon and B.C. Dungeness crab for the recipe included in this book. Making use of traditional Japanese techniques and Canadian flavours, the result is something fresh and new—and irresistible.

Togarashi spice blend

1½ Tbsp shichimi togarashi

1 Tbsp Old Bay Seasoning

1½ tsp cayenne

1½ tsp brown sugar

1½ tsp lemon pepper

1½ tsp garlic powder

Iwa nori butter

2½ Tbsp chopped tosaka ao seaweed (see Tip)

2½ Tbsp chopped tosaka aka seaweed (see Tip)

2 Tbsp chopped wakame seaweed (see Tip)

2 Tbsp aonori flakes

2 Tbsp tamari soy

2 Tbsp yuzu juice

1 cup unsalted butter

Togarashi-spiced lobster

2 Tbsp salt, plus extra to season

1 lobster (1½–2 lbs)

20 creamer potatoes

2 cobs of corn, husked and quartered

2 bunches green kale, blanched

1 cup unsalted butter, melted

2 Tbsp Togarashi Spice Blend

Juice of 1 lemon

 The seaweeds, like most of the ingredients in this recipe, can be found at Asian grocers. They can be replaced with ½ cup mixed seaweed.

 Serves 2

Togarashi-Spiced Lobster

Togarashi spice blend Combine all ingredients in a small bowl and set aside.

Iwa nori butter Combine all ingredients in a medium bowl, use a rubber spatula to fold, and mix well. Place mixture in a ramekin and set aside.

Togarashi-spiced lobster Preheat the oven to 350°F.

Fill a large saucepan two-thirds full with water and add 2 Tbsp of salt (it should taste close to ocean water). Bring water to a strong boil on high heat.

Pick up live lobster by holding the upper side (behind the head) between your thumb and middle finger. Carefully and quickly place lobster, head first, into the pot and completely submerge. Cover, return to a boil, and cook for 8 to 10 minutes.

Meanwhile, bring another large pot of water to a boil and season with salt. Add potatoes and boil for 7 minutes. Leaving potatoes in, add corn and boil for another 2 minutes. Drain and place in a large bowl.

Using tongs, remove lobster, place in another large bowl, and set aside for 5 minutes to cool.

Cut lobster in half lengthwise, then crack the claws to expose the flesh.

Place lobster and kale in the bowl with the corn and potatoes. Pour butter over top, season with togarashi spice blend, and mix.

Transfer lobster and vegetables to a large cast-iron frying pan and arrange so ingredients fill the whole pan. Bake for 5 minutes, until hot. (Be careful not to overcook.) Meanwhile, melt iwa nori butter in the microwave.

To finish, drizzle lobster and vegetables with lemon juice and serve with iwa nori butter for dipping.

Wasabi–English pea purée

½ cup water
½ cup fresh or frozen English peas
1 tsp olive oil
1 tsp good-quality soy sauce
2 tsp wasabi paste

Spiced kale chips

4 leaves cavolo nero
1 Tbsp olive oil
Salt
1 tsp shichimi togarashi

Dungeness crab tartare filling

7 oz Dungeness crabmeat, shell
　　pieces and cartilage removed
1 Tbsp mayonnaise
1 Tbsp chopped capers
1 Tbsp chopped shallots
1 Tbsp fresh lemon juice

Salmon

12 oz sashimi-grade skinless
　　sockeye salmon
¼ cup olive oil
½ cup good-quality soy sauce

Assembly

3 Tbsp ikura (salmon roe)
3 Tbsp blanched English peas
4 Tbsp (handful) fresh pea tips
4 cauliflower florets, thinly sliced

 Serves 2

Aburi Sockeye Salmon Sashimi with Dungeness Crab Tartare

Wasabi–English pea purée Pour water into a small saucepan and bring to a boil on medium heat, then add peas and blanch for 2 minutes. Place peas and water in a blender, add remaining ingredients, and blend until smooth. Scoop purée into a glass bowl, cover, and refrigerate for 1 hour, until cold.

Spiced kale chips Preheat the oven to 350°F. Place cavolo nero in a bowl, drizzle with olive oil, and add a pinch of salt. Toss to coat.

Place cavolo nero on a baking sheet and bake for 10 minutes, or until crispy (take care not to burn it). Sprinkle with shichimi togarashi and set aside to cool. Break into 2-inch pieces.

Dungeness crab tartare filling Combine all ingredients in a bowl and mix well.

Salmon Preheat a charcoal grill or non-stick frying pan on medium heat. Fill a large bowl with ice-cold water.

Rub salmon with olive oil and grill, or flash-sear, for 10 seconds on one side. Flip and sear for another 10 seconds. Transfer salmon to the bowl of water and chill until cold. Drain and pat dry with paper towels. Slice horizontally across the grain into ¼-inch pieces.

Lay salmon pieces out flat. Place 2 tsp of crab tartare at one end, and roll salmon around the tartare. Brush each piece with a little bit of soy sauce. Set aside.

To assemble On a 10-inch round plate, spread wasabi–English pea purée in a long brush-stroke motion. Place 5 pieces of salmon roll on top of purée. Spoon a little ikura on each roll. Garnish plate with kale chips, peas, pea tips, and cauli-flower slices.

Nana
Restaurant
Monte Wan

WITH THE STONE FLOORS, plastic stools, artfully weathered shutters, Thai flag bunting criss-crossing the ceiling, and monsoon-like weather on this late summer night, it's difficult to tell whether we're dining on a side street in Bangkok or at an exciting Thai restaurant on Queen Street West. Monte Wan, the owner and executive chef behind Toronto's Nana and Khao San Road, says it's all by design. "Khao San Road is like a greatest hits list of Thai cuisine," he explains. "We try to be very accommodating and to take care of everyone: pick your spice level, choose your meat, opt for a vegan or gluten-free menu. Because of the restaurant's success, I was able to venture out with Nana." The result is bolder and more intense; the dishes are pungent, fiery, adventurous, and wonderfully less accommodating. Nana's version of *khao soi* features a deeper yet lighter broth, fewer noodles, and more fresh toppings. The papaya salad, which is nose-clearing spicy, boasts an extra dose of funky fish sauce. The chicken *laab* are like crunchy chicken poppers tossed with shallots, chilies, mint, and palm sugar, and perfectly paired with a beer, while the amped-up chicken satay skewers and the pork and crab spring rolls are as familiar as they are exotic.

½ cup dried wood ear mushrooms

½ cup (1 oz) dry cellophane noodles

8 oz ground pork

½ cup finely grated carrot

¼ cup canned crab meat, drained

½ tsp salt

2 tsp granulated sugar

½ tsp freshly ground black pepper

1 Tbsp fish sauce

8 large rice paper wrappers (about 9 inches in diameter)

Canola or vegetable oil, for frying

Sweet chili dipping sauce, to serve

To make extra-crispy spring rolls, increase the oil temperature to high heat. Carefully lower the rolls into the oil and deep-fry again for 1 minute. Using a slotted spoon, transfer rolls to a plate lined with paper towels to drain.

 **Makes 8 rolls**

Vietnamese-Style Pork and Crab Spring Rolls

Soak mushrooms in a bowl of warm water for 30 minutes. Drain and set aside.

Soak cellophane noodles in a bowl of cold water for 30 minutes. Drain and roughly chop into 1½-inch pieces.

In a medium bowl, combine all ingredients except for rice paper wrappers and mix thoroughly.

Fill a roasting pan halfway with hot water, add a rice paper wrapper, and submerge until the entire sheet is wet. Remove rice paper, place onto a clean chopping board or counter, and let dry slightly. Lightly dab with paper towel if it's too wet.

Place a ¼ cup of filling in the centre of the paper, shaping it into a log and leaving a 1¼-inch margin around the edge. Working quickly, fold the bottom edge of the paper up so that it covers the entirety of the filling. Tuck the left and right sides inward toward the centre, and then roll to finish. Avoid air pockets inside the roll by rolling as tightly as possible without splitting the rice paper. Repeat with remaining wrappers and filling.

Pour oil into a saucepan to a depth of 2 inches. Warm oil on medium-high heat until it reaches 350°F. (Alternatively, use a deep fryer.) Working in batches, carefully lower the rolls into the pan and deep-fry for 2 minutes, until crisp but not browned. Turn rolls and deep-fry for another 3 minutes, until golden brown and cooked through. Using a slotted spoon, transfer rolls to a plate lined with paper towels. Serve with sweet chili dipping sauce.

Chicken satay

6 cloves garlic

2 whole Thai dried chilies (prik haeng)

2 stalks fresh lemongrass

2 cilantro roots

2 discs palm sugar

1 small shallot

1½ cups coconut milk

3 Tbsp fish sauce

3 tsp fresh turmeric

3 tsp galangal

2 tsp sea salt

1 tsp wild ginger

1 tsp ground cinnamon

2 lbs boneless chicken thighs, cut into 1½-inch long pieces

16–18 7-inch wood skewers

Peanut sauce

3 whole dried chili peppers

½ whole star anise

½ tsp ground cinnamon

¼ tsp coriander seeds

⅛ tsp black peppercorns

½ cup + 2 Tbsp roasted peanuts, divided

2½ Tbsp granulated sugar

1 tsp salt

1 cup coconut milk

1 Tbsp white vinegar

1 Tbsp vegetable oil

 **Makes 16 skewers**

Chicken Satay Skewers

Chicken satay Place all chicken satay ingredients except for chicken into a food processor and blend until smooth.

Place chicken in a large bowl, add marinade, and mix well. Cover and refrigerate for 4 hours.

Peanut sauce Combine chili peppers, star anise, cinnamon, coriander seeds, and black peppercorns in a frying pan and roast on medium heat for 1 minute, or until fragrant. Remove from the heat and transfer spices to a mortar (or food processor) and grind until almost smooth. Add ½ cup peanuts, sugar, and salt and grind until smooth.

Place ground mixture into a small saucepan, add coconut milk, vinegar, and vegetable oil and mix thoroughly until well combined. Cook sauce on medium heat for 3 to 5 minutes, or until browned and reduced by a quarter. Set aside to cool, transfer to a serving bowl, and chill in the fridge for at least 30 minutes.

To assemble Set a grill on high heat. Crush remaining 2 Tbsp of peanuts and add to the sauce. Thread a piece of chicken onto each of the presoaked wooden skewers. Place chicken skewers on grill and cook for 1½ minutes. Flip skewers and cook for another 2 minutes, until cooked through. Transfer chicken skewers to a platter and serve immediately with peanut sauce.

FACING: Chicken Satay Skewers, with Vietnamese-Style Pork and Crab Spring Rolls

Nota Bene
David Lee

"CHANGE IS IMPORTANT," says Nota Bene chef and co-owner David Lee. "Because we've been here seven years, we wanted to give back to our clientele in the sense that we want them to feel more comfortable, and feel better." To that end, designers +tongtong led a pastoral refresh of the space with clever turns like tumbleweed mounted on the dining room's ceiling and a dangly kelp-inspired leather wine rack. But the main change is to the menu, which now includes many plant-based dishes (100 percent animal-free, including no eggs and dairy) such as a delectable summer tomato and young Thai coconut ceviche and pulled barbecued mushrooms with rapini, peppers, and dandelion. "It's easy to cook great steaks, fish, or seafood and put it at the centre of the plate,"

says Lee. "That's second nature for us." To create a plant-based menu, he had to think about food differently and draw inspiration everywhere—from his childhood spent eating veg-centric Chinese dishes to his years spent working at Mosimann's in London, where he discovered *cuisine naturelle* and learned to enhance the natural flavours in cooked ingredients without the use of oil, butter, cream, or alcohol. Revolutionary back then, the techniques are evident today in the chef's fresh takes and even the offerings at the bar, like tempura wild mushrooms and jerked carrots—with cocktails to match. Feel good food, indeed.

8 sidestripe prawns, peeled and deveined

1 zucchini

1 Tbsp soy sauce

½ Tbsp green onions, finely sliced

⅓ bird's-eye chili, seeded and finely sliced

Juice of ½ lime

½ Tbsp cilantro leaves

2 Tbsp olive oil

2 shiso leaves, torn

½ nori sheet, toasted

4 wild raw chanterelles

 Serves 2

Spiral Zucchini and Prawn Salad, Chanterelles, and Chili Oil

Bring a small saucepan of salted water to a boil, add prawns, and cook for 2 minutes. Using a slotted spoon, transfer prawns to a bowl of ice water to cool. Drain and set aside.

Using a spiralizer, spiralize zucchini and divide between 2 plates. Place 4 prawns on each plate on top of zucchini.

In small bowl, combine soy sauce, green onions, chili, lime juice, and cilantro and mix well. In a small saucepan on medium heat, warm olive oil until heated through, then add olive oil to the bowl to make hot chili oil. Drizzle mixture onto the two plates and top with shiso leaf and toasted nori. Finish with chanterelles.

8 oz sashimi-grade tuna,
    cut into ¼-inch cubes
½ rib celery, finely diced
¼ avocado, cored, peeled, and
    chopped
1 Tbsp finely chopped shallots
1 sprig parsley, chopped
2 tsp sesame oil
¼ cup coarsely chopped capers

¼ cup toasted pine nuts
¼ cup crema or sour cream
2 Tbsp Scotch bonnet sauce,
    or other spicy chili sauce
4 lemon wedges
¼ cup chopped pickled ginger
Maldon sea salt
Extra-virgin olive oil

 Serves 4

NB Tuna Tartare

In a bowl, combine tuna, celery, avocado, shallots, parsley, and sesame oil and gently mix. (Do not overwork.) Taste and add more sesame oil, if necessary.

Using a 2- or 3-inch ring mould, place tuna mixture onto 4 plates, just slightly off centre. Place capers in a small pile next to the tuna. Repeat with pine nuts. Add a dollop each of crema or sour cream and Scotch bonnet or chili sauce.

Garnish the plate with a lemon wedge and pickled ginger. Finish tuna with Maldon sea salt and a drizzle of olive oil. Mix tuna with the surrounding ingredients to each guest's preference and squeeze fresh lemon juice over top.

One Restaurant

Darby Piquette

DARBY

MARK McEWAN'S CULINARY outpost in Toronto's Hazelton Hotel—a Yabu Pushelberg—designed destination of rich woods, textured walls, deep chairs, and moody neutrals—is the place to be seen in Yorkville, the lapdog capital of Canada, especially so on the hedged patio, illuminated with candlelight and buzzy chatter. Chef de cuisine Darby Piquette dishes out ingredient-driven cuisine, which runs from appetizer spoons of butter braised lobster (I once inhaled these so fast the waiter thought he'd forgotten to serve them) to foie gras mousse. There are also deeply satisfying mains like PEI grass-fed tenderloin sided by a winning twist on chimichurri sauce. In fact, Piquette loves the sauce so much he's renamed

it Darbichurri. "It's perfect for all grilled meats and seafood," says the chef, who explains that his favourite dinner during the summer is a charcoal-grilled rib-eye, grilled half lobster, garlic bread, and Caprese salad. "I pour this sauce all over my plate. It adds a wicked zing to everything." The mostly Quebec cheese lineup is an especially proud Canadian moment, but so is the s'mores sundae. One of the godfathers of Toronto's modern dining scene, McEwan creates food and places with staying power, and we owe him thanks for a handful of restaurant institutions, from North 44 to Bymark. One is just one of them.

FACING: Lobster with Citrus-Roasted Potatoes, Grilled Lemon, and Darbichurri

Citrus-roasted potatoes

4 lbs German butterball potatoes, new potatoes, or fingerlings, peeled
1½ cups fresh lemon juice
½ cup olive oil
9 cloves garlic, chopped, divided
3 Tbsp dried oregano
2 Tbsp kosher salt
¼ cup fresh thyme leaves
3 cups chicken stock
2 Tbsp vegetable oil
2 Tbsp chopped flat-leaf parsley

Herb and garlic rub

1 cup olive oil
¼ cup chopped garlic
1 Tbsp chopped fresh thyme
1 Tbsp chopped flat-leaf parsley
1 Tbsp kosher salt
1 tsp freshly ground black pepper
Juice and zest of 1 lemon

Darbichurri sauce

1 cup firmly packed flat-leaf parsley, finely chopped
2 Tbsp finely chopped shallot
1 Tbsp firmly packed basil leaves, finely chopped
2 Tbsp chopped pickled hot peppers
Zest of 3 lemons
3 cloves garlic, chopped
⅔ cup red wine vinegar
½ cup extra-virgin olive oil
¼ cup fresh lemon juice
2 Tbsp kosher salt
1 tsp smoked paprika
½ tsp freshly ground black pepper

 Serves 8

Lobster with Citrus-Roasted Potatoes, Grilled Lemon, and Darbichurri

Citrus-roasted potatoes Preheat the oven to 350°F. Place potatoes in a deep roasting pan. (Use two, if necessary, to avoid overcrowding).

In a medium bowl, combine lemon juice, olive oil, about two-thirds of the garlic, oregano, salt, thyme, and chicken stock and whisk until well mixed. Pour mixture over potatoes, and cover the roasting pan with foil. Bake for 1½ hours, or until fork-tender. Let potatoes cool in braising liquid. (They'll taste better if you let them cool overnight.) Drain potatoes, reserving 2 Tbsp of braising liquid.

Heat vegetable oil in a frying pan on medium. Add potatoes, working in batches if necessary, and sauté until browned. Stir in parsley, remaining garlic, and reserved braising liquid.

Herb and garlic rub Combine all ingredients in blender and blend until smooth.

Darbichurri sauce In a mixing bowl, combine parsley, shallots, basil, hot pepper, lemon zest, and garlic. Stir vigorously for 1 minute, or until the ingredients begin to release their natural juices. Add remaining ingredients and mix well. Allow to sit for half an hour so ingredients can get familiar with each other.

Grilled lobster
3 Nova Scotia lobsters (2½ lbs each)
Herb and Garlic Rub (see here)
3 lemons, halved and seeds removed

Grilled lobster Bring a large pot of water to a boil, gently lower in lobsters, and boil for 6 minutes, or until lobsters are bright red. (Cook lobsters in batches to avoid overcrowding.) Transfer lobsters to a bowl of ice water and set aside to soak until fully chilled.

Cut lobsters in half, lengthwise, from head to tail. Scoop out green guts and rinse lobsters under cold running water. Use a mallet to crack the claws. Brush lobster shells and meat with a generous amount of herb and garlic rub.

Preheat a charcoal grill. Place lemons, flesh-side down, onto the grill and cook for 2 minutes or until charred. Remove lemons and place them on a serving platter. Place lobsters on the grill, flesh-side down, and cook for 2 minutes. Flip over, brush with more rub, and cook for another 2 minutes. Transfer lobsters to the serving platter and serve immediately with roasted potatoes and Darbichurri. Add grilled corn, cherry tomatoes, and garnish with micro basil leaves, as desired.

Mousse

2 Tbsp vegetable oil

2 Tbsp chopped garlic

1 cup chopped shallots

1 bay leaf

2 Tbsp chopped fresh thyme

1½ cups port

5 eggs

1 lb 7 oz cold chicken livers

3½ oz cold foie gras

1 cup unsalted butter, melted

2 Tbsp sherry vinegar

2 Tbsp brandy

4 tsp salt

1 tsp freshly ground black pepper

½ tsp pink curing salt

⅛ tsp nutmeg

⅛ tsp ground allspice

 Serves 6

Foie Gras and Chicken Liver Mousse with Onion Marmalade

Mousse Preheat the oven to 300°F. Heat vegetable oil in a small saucepan on medium. Add garlic, shallots, bay leaf, and thyme and cook for 5 minutes, or until shallots are translucent. Add port and cook for another 10 minutes, or until port has reduced down to a thick syrup. Set aside and allow to cool to room temperature.

In a blender, combine port mixture and remaining ingredients and blend until smooth. Pour mixture into 6 sterilized 1-cup Mason jars and place the jars in a deep baking dish. Fill the baking dish with hot water until it is halfway up the sides of the jars. Cover the dish with aluminum foil and bake for 35 to 40 minutes, until the internal temperature of the mousse is 165°F (or until it starts to soufflé and has firmed up in the middle like a crème brûlée.) Set aside to cool, then seal Mason jars with lids. Chill overnight in the fridge. (Mousse will last up to 1 week.)

Onion marmalade

3 Tbsp vegetable oil

4 cups pearl onions, peeled and quartered

6 cloves garlic, chopped

2 Tbsp chopped fresh thyme

2 Tbsp chopped fresh rosemary

2 Tbsp salt

1 tsp freshly ground black pepper

1 cup sherry

1 cup sherry vinegar

1 cup red wine vinegar

2 cups maple syrup

Assembly

2 Tbsp vegetable oil

1 cup sage leaves

Kosher salt

Extra-virgin olive oil, for brushing

1 white baguette or sourdough, sliced (see Tip)

Sea salt and freshly ground black pepper

Aged balsamic vinegar

One uses baguette slices at the restaurant so this dish is easy to share, or pass around for hors d'oeuvres. The foie gras mousse can also be served directly from the jar, topped with onion marmalade and a side of your favourite grilled bread. The onion marmalade, which can be refrigerated for up to a week, can be added to a cheeseboard or on top of baked brie.

Onion marmalade Heat vegetable oil in a saucepan set on medium. Add onions and sauté for 10 minutes, until onions are translucent. Add garlic, thyme, rosemary, salt, and black pepper and cook for another few minutes, until garlic is translucent. Pour in sherry and vinegars and cook for 20 minutes. Add maple syrup and cook for another 20 minutes, or until thick. Set aside.

To assemble Heat vegetable oil in a frying pan on medium. Carefully lower in sage leaves. (They should dance when added to the oil.) Fry for roughly 1 minute, or until sage turns a dark green. Using a slotted spoon, transfer sage to a plate lined with paper towels. Season with salt.

Preheat a charcoal grill or broiler. Brush olive oil onto both sides of each baguette slice and season with salt and pepper. Grill baguettes for 30 seconds, until lightly charred. Flip over and grill for another 30 seconds. Scoop a generous spoonful of mousse onto a crostini, then top with warm onion marmalade. Garnish with a fried sage leaf and a sprinkle of sea salt and top with a drizzle of balsamic vinegar. Serve immediately.

Pai Northern Thai Kitchen

Nuit Regular

THIS IS A STORY that begins atop an elephant in Southeast Asia, where Nuit and Jeff Regular fell head over tusks in love. She cooked for him, making incredible soups, curries, and street food, and, soon after, the two opened a food stall in Thailand, impressing backpackers and locals alike. Then Canada beckoned, and so it is that we find ourselves in an agreeably ramshackle room a few steps below Toronto's Duncan Street, where the look is curry shack chic, and the Regulars serve up authentic Northern Thai food. Over the years their restaurant empire has grown to include several SukhoThai locations, Sabai Sabai, and Pai Northern Thai. The base notes for Thai food are hot, sour, salty, and sweet, and when in perfect harmony, there's nothing better. Such is the case with Chef Regular's pomelo salad—the citrus fruit is tossed with coconut, roasted peanuts, chili, tiger shrimp, lemongrass, and cilantro and spirited away in a tart lime fish sauce and a coconut sugar dressing. Her chicken pad Thai is the kind made from tamarind paste, not ketchup, hence its savoury appeal. Have I mentioned the annual in-restaurant water fight? Super-soakers and Chiang Mai beef noodle soup for all!

Sauce

2 Tbsp fish sauce

2 Tbsp fresh lime juice

2 Tbsp coconut sugar

Salad

¼ cup toasted coconut, plus more for garnish

¼ cup coarsely ground roasted peanuts

2 Tbsp ground roasted dried shrimp

½ tsp roasted chili powder

1½ cups pomelo pulp (pulp segments broken into bite-size pieces)

8 black tiger shrimp, poached

2 Tbsp thinly sliced fresh lemongrass

2 Tbsp chopped sawtooth or long-leaf coriander

 Serves 4

Pomelo Salad

Sauce In a small bowl, mix ingredients together and set aside.

Salad In a medium mixing bowl, combine coconut, peanuts, dried shrimp, and chili powder together and mix well. Add pomelo, shrimp, lemongrass, and coriander and gently stir to combine. Add sauce and toss lightly.

To serve, place pomelo salad into a large serving dish and garnish with toasted coconut.

Tamarind paste

4 cups water

1 package (1 lb) seedless tamarind, broken into small pieces

Pad Thai sauce

1 cup water

1 cup Tamarind Paste (see here)

1 cup grated palm sugar

¼ cup fish sauce

Chicken pad Thai

⅓ cup canola oil

1 tsp minced shallot

1 tsp chopped pickled white radish

½ cup thinly sliced chicken breast

¼ cup diced firm tofu

7 oz rice noodles (about ¼-inch wide), soaked in room-temperature water for 4 hours

¾ cup Pad Thai Sauce (see here)

2 Tbsp Thai oyster sauce

2 eggs

2 Tbsp ground dried shrimp

½ cup beansprouts

¼ cup chopped Chinese chives (pieces should be about 2 inches long)

Sea salt

Brown sugar

Assembly

2 Tbsp ground roasted peanuts, for garnish

Chili powder, for garnish

1 lime wedge, for garnish

Chopped chives and beansprouts, for garnish

 Serves 2

Chicken Pad Thai

Tamarind paste In a medium saucepan on medium heat, combine water and tamarind and boil gently for 3 minutes. Cool, then strain to remove fibres. (Tamarind paste can be refrigerated up to 3 days.)

Pad Thai sauce In a saucepan on medium heat, combine water, tamarind paste, and sugar. Bring to a boil on high heat. Reduce heat to medium-low and simmer for 2 minutes.

Reduce heat to low, add fish sauce, and simmer for 1 minute. Set aside to cool. (The sauce keeps for up to 1 month in a sterile jar.)

Chicken pad Thai Heat canola oil in a large frying pan on medium. Stir in shallots and radish and cook for 10 seconds, or until fragrant. Add chicken and tofu and increase heat to medium-high. Stir in noodles and cook for another 30 seconds. Add pad Thai sauce and oyster sauce, mix well, and cook for another 2 minutes, until noodles are soft and shiny. Reduce heat to low, push noodles to one side of the pan, and add eggs to the centre of the pan, lightly breaking them up with a wooden spoon. Cover eggs with noodles and toss for 1 minute, until eggs are cooked through. Stir in dried shrimp, beansprouts, and chives and mix well. Taste and adjust seasoning with sea salt and a pinch of brown sugar.

To assemble Mound noodles into a large serving dish and garnish with ground roasted peanuts and chili powder. Place lime wedge on the side of the plate and serve with a bowl of beansprouts and chives.

Patois
Craig Wong

COME FOR THE crave-worthy Chinese/Jamaican/French creations and stay for chef and owner Craig Wong's winning smile. It further warms the *irie* vibe of the raucous and colourful Dundas Street room, where Wong knows what people want to eat—be it a blowout brunch of his famous fried chicken and waffles smothered in blonde butter syrup (his equally celebrated jerk chicken is served by night) or pulled oxtail grilled cheese sandwiches. An original ethnic hybrid that leans into Toronto's West Indian roots, Patois's popular appetizers and sides include Wong's take on Jamaican patties and slaw, and then veer into *Jamaisian* dishes, including jerk chicken chow mein and the Chinese "pineapple" bun burger, which is stacked with two flattop-grilled smash-burgers, oyster sauce, mayo, hickory sticks, and pickled cucumbers. (It works.) Topping the list on a menu of true originals are his shrimp balls with C-Plus *gastrique*. "Growing up, we'd go to the Chinese buffet and my favourite combination was eating the stuffed crab claw while drinking C-Plus," says Wong. Years later, he would cross-pollinate these flavours by creating deep-fried scallop and shrimp balls with a sweet and sour orange soda dipping sauce for a perfect marriage of culinary showmanship *and* childhood indulgence. And here comes that smile again.

Shawarma sauce

1 large or 2 small heads high-quality Ontario garlic, peeled and roughly chopped
½ red Scotch bonnet pepper, seeded and deveined
2 Tbsp rice vinegar
2 ice cubes, plus more if needed
1 Tbsp kosher salt
2 cups canola oil

Saltfish cake

2 large potatoes
3 lbs salt cod, soaked for 8 hours, water changed twice
6 green onions, sliced
3 cloves garlic, chopped
1 red chili, seeded and finely diced
½ red pepper, finely diced
2 egg yolks
¼ cup Kewpie mayonnaise
Salt
2 Tbsp rice flour
Butter (optional)

Court-bouillon

2 lemons, halved
2 onions
3 Tbsp black peppercorns
2 cups white wine
12½ cups water

Piperade

2 red peppers
3 sprigs fresh thyme
1 small clove garlic, chopped
½ red onion
½ cup extra-virgin olive oil
2 Tbsp rice vinegar
1 Tbsp salt
1 Tbsp sugar

Assembly

1 can (19 oz) ackee, drained
3 sprigs fresh tarragon, leaves only
Mixed pickled vegetables

 **Makes 16 cakes**

Ackee 'n' Saltfish Cakes

Shawarma sauce In a chilled food processor bowl, combine garlic, pepper, vinegar, ice cubes, and salt and process until smooth. With the food processor still running, gradually add canola oil and mix until emulsified. (If mixture becomes too warm or thick, add more ice.) Season with additional salt, if desired.

Saltfish cake and Court-bouillon Preheat the oven to 425°F.

Place potatoes on a baking sheet and bake for 50 to 60 minutes, or until fork-tender.

Meanwhile, make the court-bouillon. Combine all ingredients in a large pot and bring to a boil on high heat. Reduce heat to medium and simmer for 20 minutes.

Add cod to the pot and simmer for 10 to 12 minutes, until flaky. Using a slotted spoon, transfer cod to a cutting board and, when cool enough to handle, shred. Set aside.

In a large bowl, combine green onions, garlic, chili, and red pepper and mix together. Using a ricer, rice potatoes into the bowl, while they are still warm. (Alternatively, use a masher.) Add cod, egg yolks, mayonnaise, and salt and mix in rice flour.

Scoop about a ¼ cup of the mixture into your hands and form a patty. Repeat with remaining mixture.

In a non-stick frying pan on medium heat (or on a buttered griddle), cook the saltfish cakes, in batches, for 3 to 4 minutes. Flip and cook for another 3 to 4 minutes, until golden and cooked through.

Piperade Preheat a grill or broiler and char red peppers for 12 to 15 minutes, or until almost black. Place peppers in a bowl, wrap tightly with plastic wrap, and set aside for 15 minutes. Peel, seed, and chop the peppers.

Place peppers in a bowl, add remaining ingredients, and mix well. Place mixture in a saucepan and warm on low heat. Set aside.

To assemble Steam ackee on a plate in a bamboo steamer for 2 to 3 minutes, being careful not to break them. Spread shawarma sauce on your serving plate and place saltfish cakes on top. Add piperade and ackee, and garnish with tarragon and pickled vegetables.

C-Plus gastrique
2 cups orange soda, such as C-Plus
2⅓ cups Chinese red vinegar

Bay scallop and shrimp balls
1 lb black tiger shrimp, peeled,
  deveined, and chopped, divided
¼ lb bay scallops
1½ Tbsp Shaoxing rice wine
1½ Tbsp + ¼ cup cornstarch, divided
1 tsp sesame oil
1½ Tbsp salt
¼ tsp ground white pepper
4 cups panko crumbs
Vegetable oil, for deep-frying
Red chili slices, for garnish
Thai basil leaves, for garnish

 **Serves a crowd**

Bay Scallop and Shrimp Balls with C-Plus Gastrique

C-Plus gastrique Pour soda into a small saucepan, bring to a boil, then lower to a simmer on low heat until reduced by three-quarters. Add vinegar and cook for another 10 minutes, until reduced further and slightly thickened. (You should have about 1½ cups.) Set aside.

Bay scallop and shrimp balls Place a food processor bowl and blade in the freezer and leave for 30 minutes.

Remove the equipment, add half of the shrimp to the bowl, and pulse quickly 3 times. Chop remaining shrimp. Place all of the shrimp and scallops in a bowl, add rice wine, 1½ Tbsp cornstarch, sesame oil, salt, and pepper, and mix well.

Cook a small amount of the mixture in a frying pan on medium to test for seasoning. Adjust if necessary.

Dip your hands in water, scoop mixture in your hands, and form into golf ball–sized balls. Set aside.

Place panko on a plate. In a small bowl, mix ¼ cup cornstarch with 2 cups of water and stir. Working in batches, lightly dip shrimp balls into the cornstarch mixture. Transfer the balls to the panko and coat well.

Heat vegetable oil in a deep fryer or deep saucepan on medium, until it reaches a temperature of 325°F. Gently lower shrimp balls into the oil and deep-fry for 4 minutes, or until they reach an internal temp of 135°F. Using a slotted spoon, transfer the balls to a plate lined with a paper towels.

To serve, skewer a slice of red chili, then a leaf of Thai basil, followed by the balls. Place skewers on a serving platter (on a bed of shredded lettuce, if desired) and serve sauce on the side.

Pizzeria Libretto
Rocco Agostino

THE LIBRETTO RESTAURANT GROUP has revolutionized how Toronto enjoys its pizza (read: VPN-certified and wood-fired). And it all began with Chef Rocco Agostino's deep devotion to Neapolitan pies. Naples has a storied history of pizza-making and snacking that dates back to the 18th century, and it's the lively stands selling hot slices that Agostino sought to replicate back home on Canadian soil. Stefano Ferraro wood-fired ovens are installed at all five locations, where they bake up 90-second signature pies including the Margherita and Ndjula pizza (cayenne-infused sausage, fresh oregano and basil, garlic,

mozzarella, and stracciatella). The heart and hearth of this operation, these 950°F ovens are made from third-generation pizza makers, and everything that goes in them comes out better. Rounding out the deeply delicious dishes are arancini and meatballs and seasonal salads such as the arugula—with Piave cheese, toasted walnuts, and pears—and their heirloom caprese. After devouring them you can sit back, snap your fingers, and imagine you're suddenly in Naples.

Gamay dressing
3 cups extra-virgin olive oil
1 cup Gamay wine vinegar
½ cup honey
Salt, to taste

Salad
4 cups arugula
2 Bosc pear, sliced
¾ cup walnuts, toasted and slightly crushed
¾ cup Piave cheese, thinly sliced
¼ cup Gamay Dressing (see here)
Salt and coarsely ground pepper, to taste

 Serves 4

Arugula Salad

Gamay dressing Place ingredients into a blender and process for 1 minute, or until smooth.

Salad Mix arugula, pear, walnuts, and cheese with the dressing and add salt and pepper to taste. Put in a large bowl and serve family style.

Rocco Agostino's pizza dough

1 package (1¼ oz) active dry yeast

2⅔ cups lukewarm water, divided

2 Tbsp + ½ tsp salt

3½ cups "00" flour (see Tip)

Pizza

1 portion Dough (see here)

½ cup tomato sauce

1 Tbsp chopped basil leaves

2⅔ oz mozzarella, sliced
   (or ¾ cup grated)

1 Tbsp extra-virgin olive oil

You can find "00" flour in many Italian supermarkets or specialty baking stores. We recommend making a large batch of dough and freezing it in balls. Defrost the dough 3 to 4 hours before grilling, making sure it's at room temperature before prepping. In a pinch, store-bought dough can be used.

Serves 1 · Dough makes 6–8 balls

Margherita Pizza

Dough In a small bowl, mix yeast with approximately 2 Tbsp water.

Add remaining water and salt to the bowl of a stand mixer fitted with a dough hook attachment. Add three-quarters of the flour to the bowl and mix on low for 5 minutes. Add yeast-and-water mixture and remaining flour and mix for another 5 minutes. Let stand for 10 minutes. Restart mixer and mix for another 5 minutes.

Transfer dough to a large container with a lid and let stand for 14 hours. (Alternatively, place in a large greased bowl and cover with plastic wrap.) Divide the dough into 6 to 8 balls, depending how large you want your pizzas to be. Place in a container, covered, and let rest for 5 hours. (Dough can be stored up to 3 months in the freezer.)

Pizza Preheat the oven to 500°F. Stretch dough ball to 12 inches and place on a round stainless steel sheet pan. Using a spoon, spread tomato sauce evenly on dough, leaving a 1-inch rim around the outer edge. Add basil and mozzarella evenly over the pizza. Drizzle with olive oil and bake in the oven for 8 to 10 minutes, or until browned and bubbly.

Pusateri's
Tony Cammalleri

OVER THE PAST FIVE DECADES, Pusateri's chic flagship food shop in midtown has become synonymous with graceful grocery runs in Toronto. And thanks to a recent expansion, that experience can now be shared by anyone within reach of Bayview Village, Sherway Gardens, the Eaton Centre, and Oakville Place. I routinely meet friends for cappuccinos and pastries before picking up provisions at Saks Food Halls by Pusateri's, where a collective of Toronto's best artisanal baked goods—including Blackbird Baking Co., Forno Cultura, St. John's Bakery, Fred's Bread, and Sullivan & Bleeker—is gathered under one roof. Countless uniquely Canadian goods are on offer, and at the Sherway Gardens location, there's even a counter devoted to Mario Pingue's Niagara-made salumi. But besides the exceptional array of everyday comestibles that loyal patrons have come to love, Pusateri's offers a range of ready-made meals designed and prepared by corporate chef Tony Cammalleri, who is renowned for turning out dishes that taste homemade. (Many a fake-out dinner party meal has been made by Cammalleri and crew before being sneakily plated on the host's own serving platters.) Be it spoon-tender Barolo-braised beef cheeks with cheesy polenta, or their famous chocolate chip banana bread, this is home cooking with a giant wink.

Barolo-braised beef cheeks

2 lbs beef cheeks, cleaned, trimmed, and cut into 2-inch cubes

Sea salt and freshly ground black pepper

⅓ cup all-purpose flour

4 Tbsp olive oil, divided

5 cloves garlic, skin on

½ an onion, cut into 1-inch cubes

1 rib celery, cut into 1-inch cubes

1 small carrot, cut into 1-inch cubes

¼ cup tomato paste

24 oz Barolo or any full-bodied red wine

4 cups sodium-free beef stock

3 sprigs fresh rosemary, stemmed and finely chopped

2 sprigs fresh thyme, stemmed and finely chopped

Cheesy polenta

1 head garlic

4 cups sodium-free chicken stock

1 cup medium-coarse cornmeal flour

1 cup whipping (35%) cream

2 Tbsp unsalted butter

3 Tbsp grated Parmigiano-Reggiano

½ cup shredded Fontina

½ Tbsp chopped flat-leaf parsley

Sea salt and freshly ground black pepper

 Serves 4

Barolo-Braised Beef Cheeks with Cheesy Polenta

Barolo-braised beef cheeks Season beef with salt and pepper, then dredge in flour. Heat 2 Tbsp olive oil in a Dutch oven set on medium-high. Add beef and sear until golden on all sides. Transfer to a plate lined with paper towels.

In the same pan, heat the remaining 2 Tbsp of olive oil on medium. Add garlic, onions, celery, and carrots and sauté for 7 to 8 minutes, until golden. Add tomato paste, mix until vegetables are coated, and cook for 3 to 4 minutes. Add wine, bring to a boil, and cook for 3 to 4 minutes, until liquid is reduced by a quarter. Add beef stock and cook for another 2 to 3 minutes.

Add beef and herbs and simmer, covered, for 1½ to 2 hours, until beef is very tender. Remove the lid, reduce heat to low, and cook for another 20 minutes, until sauce has thickened to a gravy-like consistency. (If meat is too tender, scoop it out gently and reduce sauce until desired thickness is achieved, then add meat back to the pot.) Remove garlic cloves and adjust seasoning to taste.

Cheesy polenta Cut across the top of the garlic, about ¾ of an inch from the top, and bake, face-side up, for 40 minutes, or until soft. Set aside to cool, then squeeze out softened garlic onto a cutting board and finely chop until it becomes a smooth purée. (The garlic can be refrigerated in a sealed container for up to 1 week.) Set aside.

In a heavy-bottomed pot on high heat, bring chicken stock to a boil. Whisk in 1½ Tbsp of garlic purée. Reduce heat to medium-high, then gradually add cornmeal while whisking continuously. Reduce heat to medium and simmer for 10 to 15 minutes. Stir in cream.

Remove pot from the heat, add butter, cheeses, and parsley and mix well with a wooden spoon. Season with salt and pepper to taste.

To serve, divide polenta between 4 plates. Top with braised beef cheeks and wine sauce.

3½ very ripe bananas, mashed

2½ cups granulated sugar

3 eggs

1 tsp vanilla extract

½ cup sunflower oil

1 tsp ground cinnamon

1½ cups all-purpose flour

2½ tsp baking soda

½ tsp sea salt

½ cup bittersweet chocolate chips

 2 loaves

Pusateri's Chocolate Chip Banana Bread

Preheat the oven to 350°F. In a stand mixer, combine bananas, sugar, eggs, vanilla, sunflower oil, and cinnamon and mix well for 1 to 2 minutes.

In a separate bowl, sift together flour, baking soda, and salt. Gradually add the dry mixture to the wet mixture in the stand mixer and mix for 1 minute. Stir in chocolate chips.

Pour batter into 2 non-stick loaf pans and bake for 40 to 45 minutes, until a skewer inserted into the centre comes out clean. Set aside to cool and serve.

Raca Café & Bar

Ivana Raca

A BALINESE THEME with a Parkdale neighbour-hood vibe, Raca Café & Bar features Ivana Raca's casual fine-dining menu, done with precision but without pretension. Regulars stream in for seasonal winners such as warm heirloom tomato salad (the tomatoes are peeled!); tender kale salad with tamari almonds, preserved blueberries, and Parm; and fresh pappardelle with roasted mush-room cream sauce and shaved black truffle. "Mark will tell you I have the best risotto in the city," says Chef Raca. "Everything I do comes from him." She's talking about Mark McEwan (see One, page 148), her boss and mentor for 10 years before she struck out on her own. And regarding that risotto, it's as luxurious as a mink in a top hat. They cut no corners here. Everything is made in-house, and while some dishes seem simple, every ingredient has a purpose, with not a vege-table out of season. Cocktails, such as the saffron daiquiri, are also winners, and the chocolate brownie trifle will have you singing in the streets. And the Indonesian-led décor? "It's very me," Raca says. "Bali has a special place in my heart, so it's very Zen here."

Sweet apple jam

2 Tbsp unsalted butter

3 gala apples, peeled, cored, and diced

½ cup packed brown sugar

2 cups Inniskillin ice wine

1 cinnamon stick

1 star anise

3 cloves

1 tsp fresh thyme leaves

Veal bone marrow arancini

3 Tbsp canola oil, plus 4 cups for frying

1 onion, finely chopped

3 cloves garlic, finely chopped

1 cup carnaroli rice

½ cup white wine

8½ cups hot chicken stock, divided

1 Tbsp kosher salt

3 Tbsp unsalted butter

4 Tbsp grated Danish fontina

2 cups all-purpose flour

4 eggs

3 cups whole milk

3 cups panko

1 cup scooped-out veal bone marrow, frozen and cut into ½-inch cubes

Salt and freshly ground black pepper

Toasted peanuts, for garnish

3 Tbsp pinenuts, toasted, for garnish

 **Makes 25 arancini**

Veal Bone Marrow Arancini with Sweet Apple Jam

Sweet apple jam In a small saucepan on medium heat, melt butter and cook for 1 minute, until browned. Add apples and sauté for 5 minutes, until apples are soft. Add brown sugar, ice wine, cinnamon stick, star anise, and cloves, reduce heat to low, and cook for 12 minutes, until jam has reduced by half. Add thyme, stir, and set aside to cool at room temperature.

Veal bone marrow arancini Heat 3 Tbsp canola oil in a frying pan on medium-low. Add onions and sauté for 7 minutes, or until translucent. Add garlic and sauté for another minute, until fragrant. Stir in rice and toast for 2 minutes. (Toasting the rice will release the starch and make your risotto creamy.) Add wine and cook until liquid is reduced by half.

Add 2 Tbsp chicken stock and cook until the rice absorbs most of the liquid. Repeat, stirring continuously, until half the stock is used. Add salt, stir, and continue adding stock for about 19 minutes, until risotto is almost cooked. Stir in butter and fontina. Once done, spoon risotto onto a large, rimmed baking sheet and spread it out to cool.

Meanwhile, set up the breading station. Place flour into a bowl. In a separate bowl, combine eggs and milk and whisk. Place panko into a third bowl.

Wearing latex gloves, use your hands to make golf ball–sized balls using the cooled risotto. Stuff each ball with a cube of frozen veal marrow. Coat the arancini in flour, then in egg-milk wash, and finally in panko, carefully shaking off any excess. Place breaded arancini on a baking sheet and refrigerate for 1 hour, until firm.

Heat 4 cups canola oil in a deep saucepan on medium until it reaches a temperature of 350°F. To test the oil, drop in a few panko crumbs; if they sizzle and float, you are good to go. Using tongs or a slotted spoon, carefully lower 5 arancini into the oil and cook for 5 minutes, until golden. Transfer arancini to a plate lined with paper towels and drain. Season with salt and pepper and cook the remaining arancini in batches.

To serve, place arancini on a platter, garnish with toasted peanuts and pinenuts, and serve hot with a side of jam.

Garlic aioli
2 cloves garlic
Salt
1 egg yolk
2 Tbsp fresh lemon juice
¼ tsp Dijon mustard
2 cups vegetable oil
Freshly ground black pepper

Shrimp-stuffed arancini
6 cups chicken stock
½ tsp saffron threads
3 Tbsp canola oil, plus 4 cups for frying
1 onion, finely chopped
3 cloves garlic, finely chopped
1 cup carnaroli rice
½ cup white wine
1 Tbsp kosher salt
3 Tbsp unsalted butter

¼ cup grated Parmigiano-Reggiano, plus more for garnish
2 cups all-purpose flour
4 eggs
3 cups whole milk
3 cups panko
12 black tiger shrimp (13–15), peeled, deveined, and cut in half
Salt and freshly ground black pepper
Baby watercress, for garnish

 **Makes 24 arancini**

Saffron Shrimp–Stuffed Arancini with Garlic Aioli

Garlic aioli Combine garlic and a pinch of salt on a cutting board and finely chop together until a paste is formed. In a medium bowl, combine egg yolk, lemon juice, and mustard and whisk together. Gradually add oil, whisking continuously, until aioli starts to emulsify. If mixture seems too thick and starts to separate, add more lemon juice. Whisk in garlic and season with pepper and, if desired, additional salt.

Shrimp-stuffed arancini In a saucepan on high heat, combine chicken stock and saffron threads and bring to a boil, then reduce to a simmer.

Heat 3 Tbsp canola oil in a frying pan on medium-low. Add onions and sauté for 7 minutes, or until onions are translucent. Add garlic and sauté for another minute, until fragrant. Stir in rice and toast for 2 minutes. (Toasting the rice will release the starch and make your risotto creamy.) Add wine and cook until liquid is reduced by half.

Add 2 Tbsp chicken stock and cook until the rice absorbs most of the liquid. Repeat, stirring continuously, until half the stock is used. Add salt, stir, and continue adding stock for about 19 minutes, until risotto is almost cooked. Stir

in butter and Parmigiano-Reggiano. Once done, spoon risotto on a large, rimmed baking sheet and spread out to cool.

Meanwhile, set up the breading station. Place flour into a bowl. In a separate bowl, combine eggs and milk and whisk. Place panko into a third bowl.

Wearing latex gloves, use your hands to make golf ball–sized balls using the cooled risotto. Stuff each ball with a shrimp. Coat the arancini in flour, then in egg-milk wash, and finally in panko, carefully shaking off any excess. Place breaded arancini on a baking sheet and refrigerate for 1 hour, until firm.

Heat 4 cups canola oil in a deep saucepan on medium until it reaches a temperature of 350°F. To test the oil, drop in a few panko crumbs; if they sizzle and float, you are good to go. Using tongs or a slotted spoon, carefully lower 5 arancini into the oil and cook for 5 minutes, until golden. Transfer arancini to a plate lined with paper towels and drain. Season with salt and pepper and cook remaining arancini in batches.

To serve, place arancini on a serving platter, garnish with grated Parmigiano-Reggiano, and top with watercress. Serve hot with a side of aioli.

Rickshaw Bar

Noureen Feerasta

A GROUP OF VEGAN and meat-loving pals walk into a bar and discover that it's not a bar, but in fact a wondrous restaurant where they can all enjoy drinks and delicious sharable plates. This is the magic of Noureen Feerasta, who grew up in Pakistan, worked at Origin and Momofuku, and developed a feel for what Torontonians will eat (everything!) before launching her own restaurant. Rickshaw Bar takes inspiration from India and Pakistan to Burma and East Africa: Feerasta is truly a chef of the world, and the cultural familiarity shows on the plate. The Queen Street streetcar rumbling by is the only tip-off that you're still in Toronto. Beef *mishkaki* are delectable skewers of marinated steak, perked up with garlic, ginger, earthy spices, and fresh herbs. And you don't have to be vegan to love her plant-based dishes, like Brussels sprouts with green chutney, or makai curry, spun out of corn stock and cashews, the spiced broth full of grilled eggplant, zucchini, and rounds of corn cob. The delightful crispy milk pastries see milk custard hit with cardamom, wrapped in phyllo, and scattered with almonds and rose petals. Enjoy your life choices, vegans.

6 cloves garlic, peeled

1 onion, roughly chopped

4 jalapeño peppers, deseeded and roughly chopped

1 cup packed cilantro (including stems), roughly chopped, plus more for garnish

½ cup packed mint, roughly chopped

1 Tbsp vegetable oil

4 cups Brussels sprouts, trimmed and cut in half lengthwise

Salt

3 tsp fresh lime juice

¼ cup coconut cream

 Serves 4–6

Pan-Roasted Brussels Sprouts

Combine garlic, onions, jalapeño, cilantro, and mint in a food processor and process until smooth. Set aside.

Heat vegetable oil in a large frying pan on medium-high. Add Brussels sprouts, cut-side down, and sear for 3 minutes, until browned. Transfer Brussels sprouts to a plate.

In the same pan, add ¼ cup of the onion mixture and cook on medium heat for 2 to 3 minutes, until fragrant. Return Brussels sprouts to the pan, reduce heat to low, and toss. Season with salt and lime juice and toss to coat. Add coconut cream and toss again. Transfer to a serving plate, garnish with cilantro, and serve immediately.

1 tsp cumin seeds

1 tsp coriander seeds

6 cloves garlic, peeled

1 onion, roughly chopped

2-inch piece fresh ginger, peeled

½ cup packed cilantro (including stems), roughly chopped, plus more for garnish

¼ cup packed mint, roughly chopped

2 Tbsp tamarind paste

½ cup plain yogurt

3 tsp fresh lime juice

3 tsp salt

1 tsp granulated sugar

2 lbs sirloin steak, cut into 2-inch pieces

10–12 wooden skewers, soaked in water for 30 minutes

Flatbread, to serve

 Serves 4–6

Beef Mishkaki

In a frying pan on low heat, combine cumin and coriander seeds and roast until fragrant, about a minute. Using a pestle and mortar, grind into a powder.

Add garlic, onions, ginger, cilantro, mint, tamarind paste, and yogurt to a food processor and blend until smooth. Add lime juice, salt, and sugar. Transfer mixture to a non-reactive bowl, add beef, and marinate for 1 hour, covered, in the fridge.

Preheat the grill to medium-high. Thread beef onto skewers and grill steaks for 2½ minutes. Turn and cook for another 2½ minutes, until medium rare. Garnish with cilantro or mint and serve with flatbread, sliced cucumber, red cabbage, and a squirt of lime, if using.

FACING: Beef Mishkaki, with Pan-Roasted Brussels Sprouts

The Rolling Pin

Isabelle Loiacono
and Vanessa Baudanza

THE ROLLING PIN is a pretty shop on the Avenue Road strip with a modern take on 1950s nostalgia. It also has a weekly doughnut schedule, which I've just happened to enter into my computer's database. What better way to cheer up a gloomy Monday than by feasting on a PB and J, a fluffy glazed doughnut with peanut butter frosting, raspberry jam, and toasted peanuts. Hello doughnut, goodbye Monday blues! They make all sorts of indulgent treats here, including cupcakes, pop tarts, cookies, stunning cakes, macarons, pies, and squares. Best of all, co-owners and pastry chefs Vanessa Baudanza and Isabelle Loiacono have reassured us that making doughnuts at home isn't difficult—proof of which can be found in the Classic Sour Cream Doughnuts recipe featured here. "And if you love the classic chocolate chip cookie, you will especially love our squares recipe," says Baudanza. "It's the perfect spin on the cookie for a family gathering or work holiday party." Can you say, "Workplace Hero"?

Cinnamon sugar
1 cup granulated sugar
¼ cup ground cinnamon

Doughnuts
½ cup sour cream
½ cup buttermilk
½ cup granulated sugar
1 egg
½ tsp salt
1 tsp vanilla
1¾ cups all-purpose flour
1 tsp baking soda
⅛ tsp nutmeg
Vegetable oil, for frying

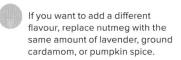
If you want to add a different flavour, replace nutmeg with the same amount of lavender, ground cardamom, or pumpkin spice.

 **Makes about 24**

Classic Sour Cream Doughnuts

Cinnamon sugar In a small bowl, mix both ingredients together and set aside.

Doughnuts In a large bowl, combine sour cream, buttermilk, sugar, egg, salt, and vanilla and whisk until mixed through. In another bowl, sift together flour, baking soda, and nutmeg. Combine dry ingredients into wet ingredients, and mix together until just blended. Set aside.

Heat 3 to 4 inches of vegetable oil in a deep fryer or deep saucepan on medium, until it reaches a temperature of 350°F. Using a small ice-cream scoop or a tablespoon, carefully drop scoops of dough into the oil, in batches, without splashing. Deep-fry for 4 minutes, or until golden brown. Turn and cook to the same colour on the other side. Using tongs or a slotted spoon, transfer doughnuts to a plate lined with paper towels and drain. Cool slightly, then roll doughnuts in cinnamon sugar. Serve warm.

Crust

1⅓ cups all-purpose flour

¼ tsp salt

2 Tbsp granulated sugar

⅓ cup unsalted butter, chilled

¼ cup whole milk

1 tsp vanilla

1 cup semi-sweet or dark chocolate chips

Filling

2 large eggs

½ cup granulated sugar

½ cup packed brown sugar

¾ cup unsalted butter, room temperature

½ cup all-purpose flour

 Makes 24 squares

Chocolate Chip Cookie Squares

Crust Preheat the oven to 325°F. Line the bottom and sides of a 9 × 13-inch baking pan with parchment paper.

Combine all dry ingredients in the bowl of a stand mixer fitted with a paddle attachment. Cube butter and add to the dry ingredients. Turn the mixer on low, mix, and gradually add in milk and vanilla. (The mixture will be very crumbly.) Transfer mixture into the baking pan, pressing down firmly and evenly along the bottom. Sprinkle chocolate chips on the top of the crust.

Filling Beat eggs in a large mixing bowl for 4 to 5 minutes on high speed until foamy. Add sugars and beat for another 2 to 3 minutes. Lower the mixer speed, add butter and flour, and mix until thick and creamy. Gently pour filling into the baking pan and spread gently with a spatula to cover all chocolate chips.

Bake for 25 to 30 minutes, or until a knife inserted halfway comes out clean. Put aside to set, preferably overnight.

Roselle Desserts

Bruce Lee and
Stephanie Duong

BRUCE

IF THIS CHEERY DESSERT SPOT in Corktown isn't the definition of a hidden gem, I'll eat one of their Earl Grey shorties (and happily, as they're tea-infused shortbreads sandwiching white chocolate and candied orange). Chef-owners Stephanie Duong and Bruce Lee had always imagined a place of their own—"where people can chill out and have great pastries," says Duong. In sharp contrast to Restaurant Régis & Jacques Marcon and yam'Tcha (the Michelin-starred restaurants in France) and Robuchon and Tim's Kitchen in Hong Kong where they worked (Bruce on the culinary arts side, Stephanie on the pastry side), Roselle has a breezy demeanour, complete with a soft-serve machine and a bench out front. But

don't let it fool you. The homemade soft-serve boasts infused cream, toasted milk powder, and injections of fresh lemon curd. There are buttery caramels and exquisite cakes, but no pies. "I don't really like pie, except for banana cream pie," says Duong. "We do a Toronto take with our Banana Cream Pie Éclair." To make them, a choux paste is covered with crunchy *craquelin*, baked, and then filled with caramelized and flambéed bananas and a whipped white chocolate ganache. "This éclair represents our philosophy at Roselle: simple flavours, a little bit of skill, and a whole lot of love." It's about exquisite pastries, for the people.

FACING: Roselle's Banana Cream Pie Éclair

Craquelin
1 cup packed brown sugar, less 1 Tbsp
¾ cup unsalted butter, room temperature
1½ cups all-purpose flour, plus more for
  dusting

Choux pastry
½ cup water
½ cup 2% milk
½ cup unsalted butter
1 tsp granulated sugar
½ tsp kosher salt
1 cup + 2 Tbsp all-purpose flour
5 eggs

Baked éclairs freeze extremely
well in an airtight container for
up to 3 months. Refresh in a
350°F oven for 10 minutes, when
needed.

The cream can be easily infused
with other flavours. Simply
replace the vanilla bean with teas
or spices in the milk infusion.

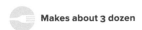 **Makes about 3 dozen**

Roselle's Banana Cream Pie Éclair

Craquelin Combine sugar and butter in the bowl of a stand mixer fitted with the paddle attachment. Beat on medium speed for 3 minutes, until creamy. Gradually add flour on low speed, until well combined. Divide dough in half.

Roll one portion between two pieces of parchment paper until ⅛ inch thick. Repeat with the other half. Transfer to a baking sheet and freeze for 20 minutes, until firm.

Remove parchment paper and transfer each portion to a lightly floured work surface. Cut each portion into 6 × 1½-inch rectangles and discard any scraps—you should have about 3 dozen portions. Freeze until ready to use.

Choux pastry Preheat the oven to 400°F (preferably on convection setting, if available). Line 4 baking sheets with parchment paper and set aside.

In a medium saucepan, combine water, milk, butter, sugar, and salt and bring to a boil on medium-high heat. Remove the pan from the heat (but keep burner on). Add flour and stir, until doughy.

Return the saucepan to the heat and cook for 5 minutes, stirring continuously, until dough is cooked through. (It should pull away from the sides of the pot, and a thin film should form on the bottom of the pot.)

Transfer dough to the bowl of a stand mixer fitted with the paddle attachment. Beat on low for 5 minutes, until slightly cooled. Add eggs, one at a time, and mix until shiny and smooth.

Transfer mixture to a piping bag fit with a star tip #32. Pipe 5½-inch long lines of dough, 2 inches apart, onto the prepared baking sheets (you should have about 3 dozen lines of dough).

Lay a piece of craquelin over each line of dough and bake for 15 minutes, until éclairs are fully puffed. Reduce the oven temperature to 350°F and bake for another 12 to 15 minutes, until evenly brown.

Vanilla pastry cream Pour milk into a medium saucepan, scrape in seeds from vanilla bean, and bring to a boil on high heat. Remove from the heat and let stand, covered, until ready to use.

Vanilla pastry cream

1 cup + 4 Tbsp 2% milk
1 vanilla bean, halved lengthwise
4 egg yolks
⅓ cup granulated sugar
3 Tbsp cornstarch
1 cup whipping (35%) cream

Whipped ganache

3 cups whipping (35%) cream, divided
14 oz white chocolate, roughly chopped

Caramelized bananas

2 cups granulated sugar, divided
6 very ripe bananas, roughly chopped
½ cup gold rum

Assembly

Icing sugar, for dusting

In a medium bowl, combine egg yolks, sugar, and cornstarch and whisk until combined. Gradually whisk 3 Tbsp hot milk into the egg mixture, then add the rest. Return mixture to the saucepan and cook, whisking constantly, on medium-high heat. Bring to a boil, and then cook for 2 minutes.

Transfer custard to a shallow bowl, cover custard surface with plastic wrap, and refrigerate for 1 hour, until cool.

Transfer cooled custard to a food processor and whirl until smooth. Transfer to a medium bowl.

Pour whipping cream into a separate bowl and whip until medium peaks form. Fold cream into custard until evenly combined, and refrigerate until chilled and you are ready to use.

Whipped ganache Pour 2 cups cream into a medium saucepan and bring to a boil on medium-high heat. Remove from the heat, then add chocolate and set aside for 5 minutes, until chocolate is almost melted. Use a hand blender to combine until homogenous and smooth. Add remaining cup of cream and blend for 1 minute, until smooth. Refrigerate for at least 5 hours before using.

Caramelized bananas Heat 1 cup sugar in a shallow pan on medium-low. Do not stir. (To prevent dark spots from forming, push the sugar around with a spatula to redistribute.) Once most of the sugar has melted, sprinkle in the remainder and cook until caramel turns a deep golden brown.

Stir in bananas until they are fully coated. Add rum. Carefully ignite using a barbecue lighter and cook for 5 minutes, until the flames dissipate and bananas have softened. Scoop bananas into a strainer and discard liquid.

To assemble Transfer ganache to the bowl of a stand mixer fitted with the whisk attachment. Whip on medium-high until medium peaks form. Transfer to a piping bag fitted with a star tip (any size will do).

Using a serrated knife, slice an éclair in half lengthwise. Spread vanilla pastry cream onto the bottom half, then add a generous portion of caramelized bananas. Pipe swirls of whipped ganache over top. Sandwich with remaining half of éclair, then dust with icing sugar. Repeat with remaining éclairs.

Earl Grey shortbread

2 cups unsalted butter, room temperature

1¼ cups icing sugar

1 tsp kosher salt

2 Tbsp Earl Grey tea leaves

Zest of 1 orange

4 cups + 2 Tbsp all-purpose flour, plus more for dusting

Whipped white chocolate ganache

¾ cup + 2 Tbsp whipping (35%) cream

2¾ cups white chocolate, roughly chopped

2 drops bergamot oil

Assembly

1 cup chopped candied orange peel

 This dough is extremely versatile and can be flavoured with other citrus zest, dried herbs, or teas.

Cookies are best kept in an airtight container. Unfilled shortbread cookies can be stored in the freezer for up to 6 months.

 Makes about 15 sandwich cookies

Roselle's Earl Grey Shortie

Earl Grey shortbread In the bowl of a stand mixer fitted with the paddle attachment, combine butter, icing sugar, salt, tea leaves, and orange zest and beat on medium speed for 5 minutes, until smooth. Add flour in two batches, scraping down the sides after each addition. Continue mixing until evenly combined. Remove dough from mixer and flatten into a disk, then wrap tightly in plastic wrap. Refrigerate for at least 2 hours, but ideally overnight.

Line two 18 × 13-inch baking sheets with parchment paper. Roll out dough on a lightly floured surface until 1½ inches thick. Using a 2-inch round cutter, cut out the cookies. Arrange dough on the prepared baking sheets and chill in fridge for at least 30 minutes.

Preheat the oven to 325°F. Bake cookies in the centre of the oven for 12 minutes, until edges are slightly golden. Set aside to cool for 5 minutes, then transfer to a rack to cool completely.

Whipped white chocolate ganache Pour cream into a medium saucepan and bring to a boil on medium-high heat. Remove from the heat, then add chocolate and set aside for 5 minutes, until chocolate is almost melted. Use a hand blender to combine, and then stir in the bergamot oil. Transfer to a shallow container, cover the surface with plastic wrap, and let sit at room temperature for 2 hours, until thickened.

To assemble Transfer ganache to piping bag fitted with a round tip with a ½-inch opening. Pipe a small round in the centre of a shortbread. Press a few pieces of chopped candied orange into the ganache and top with another shortbread. Repeat with remaining cookies.

Sanagan's Meat Locker

Peter Sanagan

PETER SANAGAN WAS a chef for many years before opening his eponymous butcher shop in Kensington Market. "I was interested in bringing the kind of local quality Ontario meat you see in restaurant kitchens to a retail level," he explains, "and cutting it in a way to help people cook it at home." Sausages are a specialty. "When you buy whole pigs, you have to figure out what to do with all the bits that are difficult to sell. We learned to make good sausages very quickly." Pigs, lambs, and goats are brought in whole, but Sanagan is especially big on pork. "It's the one animal we can use almost all of," he says. The look of the space mimics the excitement of the butcher shops of Italy and France; it's basically butchery porn.

There are the fresh cuts of protein, of course, but also roasted chickens, sandwiches, terrines, pork hocks, and a million types of bacon—which can be used to make *choucroute garnie*, a popular Alsatian dish that's easy to replicate at home. "On the next cold night, invite some friends over, put down a pot of this in the centre of the table, and serve it with a baguette, good-quality mustard, a jar of gherkins, and plenty of riesling," says Sanagan. "You'll be a star."

Rub

6 tsp salt

2 tsp ground cinnamon

2 tsp ground allspice

2 tsp freshly ground black pepper

1 tsp nutmeg

1 tsp ground cloves

Pork

3 Tbsp olive oil

3 lbs boneless, skinless pork shoulder (capocollo), tied

4 large onions, roughly chopped

6 garlic cloves, roughly chopped

4 Granny Smith apples, peeled, seeded, and quartered

2 large carrots, chopped

1 rib celery, diced

2 cups dry hard apple cider

2 cups chicken stock

Salt and freshly ground black pepper

Puréed celeriac or mashed potatoes, to serve

Bouquet garni

4 bay leaves

6 sprigs fresh thyme

6 sprigs fresh sage

 Serves 6

Pork in Cider

Rub In a small bowl, combine rub ingredients. Rub over pork, cover, and refrigerate for at least 4 hours.

Pork Preheat the oven to 350°F. Heat olive oil in a large heavy-bottomed roasting pan or enamel pot on medium-high. Add pork shoulder and sear all over to brown. Transfer to a plate and keep warm.

Reduce heat to medium, add onions, and sauté for 5 minutes, until translucent. Add garlic and cook for another minute, until fragrant. Add apples, carrots, and celery and cook for another 10 minutes, or until vegetables have lightly caramelized.

Bouquet garni Tie herbs together with kitchen string. Return pork to the pan, pour in cider, and cook for about 8 minutes, or until cider is reduced by half. Add chicken stock and bouquet garni to the pan. Bring to a simmer on medium heat, cover, and place on centre rack in the oven. Braise for 2½ to 3 hours, turning pork once during cooking.

Remove the pan from the oven and set aside to rest for 30 minutes. Transfer pork to a cutting board, remove the twine, and cover with foil and a tea towel to keep it warm while preparing the sauce.

Strain cooking liquid through a fine-mesh sieve, then push the solids through the sieve with the back of a ladle. Place liquid into a saucepan, bring to a boil, and reduce by a quarter. Season with salt and pepper to taste. (The sauce will be on the thin side.)

Slice pork and place on a serving platter. Pour sauce over pork and serve with puréed celeriac or mashed potatoes.

Spice bag

1 Tbsp juniper berries

6 bay leaves

10 sprigs fresh thyme

Choucroute

1 Tbsp unsalted butter

6 slices bacon, diced

3 large onions, sliced

4 cloves garlic, minced

1 large smoked ham hock, cut into quarters (ask your butcher to cut it on the band saw)

1 small head Savoy cabbage, shredded

2 cups fermented sauerkraut

2 cups dry white wine (e.g., riesling, gewürztraminer, or pinot gris)

4 smoked pork chops (Kassler chops)

4 pork wieners (hot dog style)

4 large smoked pork sausages (any decent brand will do)

4 weisswurst sausages (look for them in any German or Eastern European deli)

Salt and freshly ground black pepper

Boiled mini potatoes, to serve

Melted butter and chives, for garnish

 Serves 8

Choucroute Garnie

Spice bag Combine berries, bay leaves, and thyme in a cheesecloth sachet.

Choucroute In a heavy-bottomed pot on medium heat, melt butter. Add bacon, onions, and garlic and sauté for 7 minutes, until translucent. Add ham hock, reduce heat to medium-low, cover, and cook for 15 minutes. Add cabbage and cook for 10 minutes, stirring frequently, until cabbage is translucent.

Add sauerkraut, wine, and spice bag, cover, and cook for 1½ hours, until the meat on the hock is pulling away from the bone. Using tongs, transfer ham hock to a cutting board. Remove the bones and skins from the hock and return it to the pot. Add pork chops, wieners, and sausages. Cover and steam for 12 to 15 minutes.

Using tongs, transfer pork chops, wieners, and sausages to a cutting board and cut into 1-inch slices so they can be shared. Check the seasoning of the cabbage and add salt and pepper if necessary.

Discard the sachet. To serve, pile cabbage stew onto a large platter and arrange smoked meats on top. Toss potatoes in butter, salt, and chives and serve alongside the choucroute garnie. Other great accompaniments include crusty bread, gherkins, and grainy mustard.

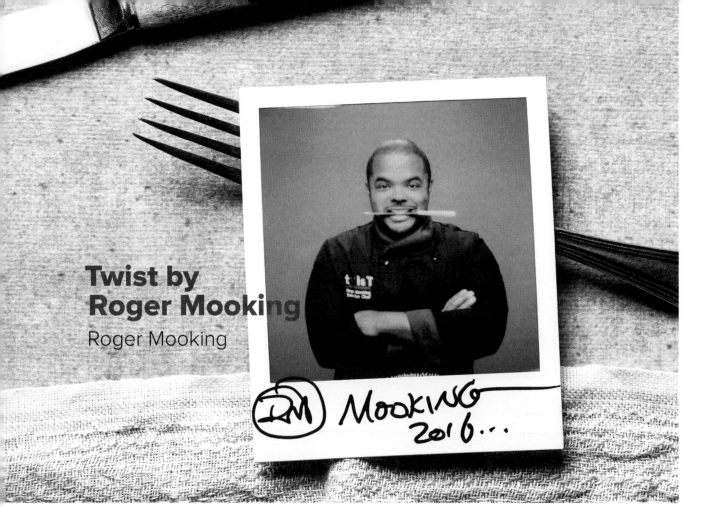

Twist by Roger Mooking

Roger Mooking

THERE'S A POSSE of chefs in Canada who come from culturally diverse backgrounds and bring with them a gleeful enthusiasm. Over the past decade, these men and women have invented a new kind of cooking we never knew we needed but now can't live without. Trinidadian-born and Edmonton-reared Roger Mooking is one of these chefs. With a smiling face recognizable from his Food Network and Cooking Channel shows (or, in a previous life, from his Juno award-winning band Bass is Base), Mooking is hard to miss. His food influences can be traced back to his family's Chinese and Caribbean kitchens as well as the Japanese, French, and Swiss German chefs he trained under. Fittingly, all of these diverse inspirations converge

at the global hub that is Toronto Pearson International Airport. Quotes such as "Feed the Soul" and "Taste the World" decorate the wood, black, and colour-burst restaurant—and the chef means it. House-made comfort foods run from snacky indulgences like short rib empanadas with chimichurri and perogies with a "twist" of chorizo and crema before moving on to fried chicken dusted with chili, topped with flash-fried basil, and served with honey lime mayo on the side. For dessert, a grilled peanut butter and jam sandwich topped with vanilla ice cream is all about fun and flavour.

Grandpa Moo's country chutney

½ cup finely sliced green onions
1 Tbsp finely diced fresh ginger
1 clove garlic, minced
⅓ cup extra-virgin olive oil
1 tsp sesame oil
¼ tsp kosher salt
Freshly ground black pepper

Lemongrass chicken

1 stalk lemongrass, top
   two-thirds trimmed off
1 chicken (2½ lbs)
2 Tbsp finely chopped
   lemongrass
1 Tbsp finely chopped garlic
2 Tbsp soy sauce
1 Tbsp Chinese cooking wine

 Serves 4

Moo's Lemongrass Chicken and Country Chutney

Grandpa Moo's country chutney Combine all ingredients in a bowl and stir well. Set aside, at room temperature, for up to 3 hours.

Lemongrass chicken Preheat the oven to 425°F. Line a rimmed baking sheet with parchment paper. Cut lemongrass in half lengthways, smash it with the back of a knife, and place it in the chicken cavity. In a small bowl, combine chopped lemongrass, garlic, soy sauce, and cooking wine and mix well. Thoroughly rub chicken inside and out with lemongrass mixture and place on baking sheet. Bake for 50 minutes, or until juices run clear. Remove from the oven and allow to rest for 5 minutes. Serve with chutney.

Roasted lamb

1 boneless lamb leg (2½ lbs)

1 Tbsp olive oil

3 Tbsp dried oregano

1½ Tbsp kosher salt

1½ Tbsp freshly ground black pepper

5 sprigs fresh rosemary

Ricotta polenta

2½ cups water

2 cups whole milk

3 cloves garlic, minced

1 cup cornmeal

3 Tbsp ricotta

Kosher salt

Freshly ground black pepper

 Serves 4–6

Roasted Lamb Leg and Creamy Ricotta Polenta

Roasted lamb Preheat the oven to 325°F. Line a rimmed baking sheet with parchment paper. Rub lamb with olive oil, oregano, salt, and pepper. Place rosemary on the baking sheet, place lamb on top, and roast for 30 minutes. Flip lamb over and baste with pan juices. Roast for another 20 minutes, or until nicely browned and tender. Remove from the oven, loosely cover with foil, and rest for 10 minutes.

Ricotta polenta In a medium pot, combine water, milk, and garlic and bring to a simmer on medium heat. Gradually whisk in cornmeal. Reduce heat to low and cook for another 8 minutes, whisking continuously, until cooked through. Remove the pot from the heat, stir in ricotta, and season with salt and pepper.

Transfer lamb to a platter and serve family style with ricotta polenta, or serve plated. Sprinkle with fresh herbs if desired.

Ufficio
Frank Venditti

THIS BEAUTIFUL RESTAURANT in Little Portugal by co-owners Jenny Coburn and Marlo Onilla—and imagined by Commute Design—is a dreamscape of brass, tile, low lighting, and close-knit tables and banquettes for group cocktailing. It's no surprise, then, that the city's designers discovered it first, clinking fennel sours as they tuck into seasonal dishes such as Ontario burrata with farro, pickled beets, and herbs, slathered over outrageously great house-made focaccia. Unique to the city, chef Frank Venditti's Italian-pescatarian menu is vibrant and light (Venditti was formerly head chef at Jamie's Italian). There's charred baby gem lettuce with roasted plums, Ontario figs, and sunflower purée, and potato gnocchi, simply and winningly sauced with pomodoro. The sustainably sourced fish and seafood crudos are the stars among the stars, while grilled octopus steals the show with a sexy risotto nero and crispy black chickpeas. Gently grilled mackerel with stracciatella cheese, marinated peppers, and Romesco sauce is a wintry delight, and one that can be replicated at home. "Mackerel is a beautiful fish but can be a bit of an acquired taste due to its oil content," says Venditti. "But the creamy, nutty, peppery purée, roasted peppers, and a unique Italian cheese balances it out."

FACING: Grilled Mackerel with Romesco Purée and Marinated Peppers, with Picante Pasini

Mackerel

2 fresh Atlantic or Spanish
mackerel, filleted and pin bones
removed by your fishmonger

Romesco purée

4 red peppers

2 tsp + ½ cup extra-virgin
olive oil, divided

Kosher salt

Freshly ground black pepper

2 cloves garlic, crushed

½ cup toasted almonds

2 Tbsp chopped flat-leaf parsley

2 Tbsp sherry vinegar

1 tsp smoked paprika

½ tsp cayenne

 Serves 2

Grilled Mackerel with Romesco Purée and Marinated Peppers

Mackerel Place mackerel skin-side down in a stainless steel pan. Refrigerate uncovered for 30 minutes, until flesh is dry and slightly firm.

Romesco purée Preheat the oven to 350°F. Line a baking sheet with parchment paper.

Place peppers in a bowl, add 2 tsp olive oil, and toss to coat. Season with salt and pepper and transfer to the prepared baking sheet. Roast for 15 minutes, remove from the oven, and place in a heatproof bowl. Cover with plastic wrap and set aside for 10 minutes.

Peel the skins off the peppers and remove seeds. Discard. Set 2 peppers aside. Place remaining 2 peppers in a blender or food processor, add garlic, almonds, parsley, sherry vinegar, paprika, and cayenne, and process until smooth. While blending, slowly add remaining ½ cup olive oil, until emulsified. Season with salt and pepper to taste.

Marinated roasted pepper
¼ cup extra-virgin olive oil, divided
1 shallot, chopped
4 cloves garlic, chopped
2 Tbsp chopped Italian parsley
2 Tbsp white wine vinegar
Sliced red chilies
Kosher salt
Freshly ground black pepper

Salad
½ cup celery leaves
1 Tbsp watercress seedlings
1 Tbsp chopped flat-leaf parsley leaves
½ Tbsp chopped chervil
½ Tbsp fresh lemon juice
1½ Tbsp extra-virgin olive oil
Salt and freshly ground black pepper

Assembly
Kosher salt
2 Tbsp olive oil
4 oz high-quality stracciatella cheese, for serving

Marinated roasted pepper Cut 2 peppers remaining from the Romesco sauce recipe into thin strips. Heat 2 Tbsp olive oil in a frying pan on medium. Add shallots and garlic and sauté for 2 minutes, until vegetables are softened and translucent. Add peppers and turn off the heat. Add parsley, vinegar, chilies, salt, and pepper and set aside for 10 minutes.

Salad In a bowl, combine all ingredients and toss to mix.

To assemble Preheat the oven to 350°F.

Heat a grill to medium-high. Season mackerel fillets with salt and oil the skin. Carefully place fish on grill, skin-side down, and cook for 30 seconds. Transfer fish to an ovenproof dish lined with parchment paper, skin-side up, and cook for 5 minutes. Remove fish from oven and let rest for 2 minutes.

Spread 2 Tbsp of Romesco purée down the centre of each plate. Season stracciatella with salt and pepper and add to the centre of the plate. Place fish on top of the cheese, add a spoonful of roasted peppers, and top with salad.

Grapefruit chili syrup

6 yellow grapefruits, segmented

3 bird's-eye chilies, seeded and deveined

Palm sugar

Picante Pasini

1½ oz Tromba Blanco

½ oz Aperol

¾ oz Grapefruit Chili Syrup (see here)

½ oz fresh lime

Bird's-eye chili, seeded and deveined, for garnish

 Serves 1

Picante Pasini

Grapefruit chili syrup Place grapefruit segments into a heavy-duty blender or food processor, add chilies and a tablespoon of water, and blend until puréed. Using a chinois or fine-mesh strainer, strain into a measuring cup and then pour into a small saucepan on medium heat. Add an equal amount of sugar as purée to the pot and heat for 10 minutes, until thickened. Remove from the heat and set aside to cool. Refrigerate until needed.

Picante Pasini Chill a stemmed cocktail coupette with ice and cold water. Set aside.

Combine ingredients in cocktail shaker, fill with crushed ice, and shake vigorously for 20 seconds, until your hands freeze. Double-strain the drink into the chilled glass and garnish with a chili on the side of the rim.

L'Unità
Miriam Echeverria

Miriam

IN TERMS OF THE Toronto restaurant scene, opening circa 2007 practically makes you an elder statesman. Yet here we are, happily ensconced amid exposed brick, flickering candles, sepia-toned lighting, and la dolce vita in upper Yorkville, feeling as youthful as ever. Still committed to thin-crust pizzas and lovingly made pastas after all these years, chef Miriam Echeverria doesn't get flustered during the heady days of TIFF, when Hollywood comes to be treated with care while sipping Barolo and slurping back fresh tagliatelle with parsnip cream and pancetta (a clever take on carbonara). Thankfully, the rest of us have all year to be treated like La La Land royalty, twirling forkfuls of Echeverria's soothing spaghetti al

pomodoro and Med-leaning mains like roasted halibut with artichoke sauce, navy beans, and olives. And those pizzas! One might be topped with mushrooms, truffle crema, roasted garlic, and fior di latte, while another is laden with potato, caramelized leeks, double-smoked bacon, and sunny-side egg for the best-ever breakfast for dinner (and dinner for breakfast the following day). It's a gentle hand making sure these beauties are thin and blistered, and the same care is taken with desserts, including the best mascarpone cannoli this side of Sicily. Long may L'Unità thrive.

FACING: Roasted Halibut with Artichoke Sauce, Navy Beans, and Infornate Olives

Vegetable stock

6 cups water

1 carrot, diced

2 ribs celery, diced

2 yellow onions, diced

1 bunch fresh thyme

½ bunch flat-leaf parsley

2 bay leaves

1 Tbsp black peppercorns

Artichoke sauce

3 Tbsp olive oil

2 large yellow onions, coarsely chopped

3 cups artichoke hearts

2 cloves garlic

4 cups Vegetable Stock (see here)

Salt and freshly ground black pepper

Navy beans

1 cup navy beans, soaked overnight and drained

1 large carrot, cut into large chunks

2 ribs celery, cut into large chunks

1 large yellow onion, halved

2 bay leaves

1 Tbsp salt

6 cups water

 Serves 4

Roasted Halibut with Artichoke Sauce, Navy Beans, and Infornate Olives

Vegetable stock In a stockpot on high heat, combine all ingredients, bring to a boil, and cook for 10 minutes. Reduce heat to medium and simmer for another 20 minutes. Strain stock and discard vegetables and herbs.

Artichoke sauce Heat olive oil in a saucepan on medium. Add onions, artichokes, and garlic, and sauté for 7 minutes, until onions are translucent. Add stock and simmer for 10 minutes, until reduced by a quarter.

Transfer mixture to a blender and purée until smooth and creamy. Season with salt and pepper. Set aside.

Navy beans In a large saucepan on medium-high heat, combine all ingredients, bring to a boil, and cook for 15 minutes. Reduce heat to medium and simmer for 30 minutes, until fully cooked. Strain beans and discard vegetables and herbs. Set aside.

Halibut

4 boneless halibut fillets (8 oz each)

Salt and freshly ground black pepper

2 Tbsp olive oil

3 shallots, minced

3 cloves garlic, minced

2 Tbsp unsalted butter

1 cup white wine

Zest of ½ a lemon

Assembly

½ cup pitted infornate olives, finely chopped, for garnish

1 bunch fresh chives, finely chopped, for garnish

Lemon juice, to garnish, and more to drizzle

Halibut Season fillets with salt and pepper. Heat olive oil in a large frying pan on high. Working in batches if necessary, add fillets and pan-fry for 3 to 5 minutes, until golden. Flip fillets and cook for another 3 to 5 minutes, until just cooked through. Transfer fillets to a plate and set aside.

In the same pan, heat a drizzle more olive oil on low. Add shallots and garlic and sauté for 2 to 3 minutes. Add butter and wine and cook for another 3 minutes, until wine has reduced and the sauce is rich and creamy. Season with salt, pepper, and lemon zest.

To assemble To serve, place navy beans in the centre of each plate. Top with a halibut fillet and dress with warm artichoke sauce. Garnish with olives and chives and add a squeeze of lemon juice plus extra artichokes if desired.

Pasta

2 cups all-purpose flour, plus
extra for dusting

2 tsp kosher salt

4 whole eggs

1 tsp olive oil

Pangrattato

2 cups vegetable oil

1 parsnip, grated

2 cups panko

 Serves 4

Parsnip Tagliatelle "Carbonara"

Pasta Combine flour and salt together on a clean surface and make a well in the centre. Add eggs and oil into the well and gently beat with a fork, slowly incorporating flour from the inside edge of the well into the eggs, mixing well until it forms a thick paste. Using a pastry scraper, fold the rest of the flour into mixture and form a dough. Fold dough onto itself and knead for 15 minutes, until it just comes together in one piece and has a smooth surface. (Do not overwork the dough.)

Place dough on a well-floured surface, wrap loosely with plastic wrap, and rest for at least 30 minutes.

Using a rolling pin, roll out dough until it's 1/16 inch thick. Divide dough into 4 equal-size sheets. Fold each sheet in half and, using a sharp knife, cut dough into ½-inch-wide ribbons. Generously dust the pasta with flour to prevent sticking. Cover and set aside for at least 15 minutes.

Pangrattato Heat vegetable oil in a frying pan on medium. Add parsnip and cook, stirring occasionally, for 7 minutes, until light golden brown. Add panko and cook for another 10 minutes, until mixture is golden brown.

Strain mixture through a fine-mesh sieve to remove excess oil, then transfer to a plate lined with paper towels to dry. (The crumbs should have a crunchy texture.) Keep in an airtight container at room temperature and use when needed.

Parsnip crema

2 Tbsp olive oil

2 large white onions, cut into ½-inch cubes

3 parsnips, cut into ½-inch cubes

½ cup unsalted butter

1 bay leaf

3 cups whole milk

Pinch of nutmeg

Salt and freshly ground black pepper

Assembly

1 cup pancetta, cut into ¼-inch cubes

2 shallots, minced

½ cup white wine

2 Tbsp flat-leaf parsley

Salt and freshly ground black pepper

Parsnip crema Heat olive oil in a large saucepan on medium-high. Add onions and sauté for 7 minutes, until translucent. Add parsnips, butter, and bay leaf, reduce heat to medium, and cook for another 5 minutes. Add milk and simmer for 10 minutes, until parsnips are soft.

Transfer everything to a blender and purée on high speed until smooth. Season with the nutmeg, salt, and pepper. Set aside.

To assemble Bring a large pot of salted water to a boil on high heat, then add pasta and cook for 2 to 3 minutes, stirring often, until pasta rises to the surface. Drain.

In a large frying pan on medium heat, render the pancetta lardons until crispy. Add shallots and cook for 3 minutes. Add white wine, cook for another 3 minutes, and reduce by half. Add parsnip crema, reduce heat to low, and warm through. Add cooked pasta, garnish with parsley and a generous amount of black pepper and salt to taste, and toss pasta until well coated.

To serve, divide pasta between 4 plates and top with pangrattato.

Verity Club
Lorenzo Loseto

CANADIAN CULINARY CHAMP and Toronto cuisine torchbearer Lorenzo Loseto has an eye for detail and whimsical creativity. Both traits befit the elegant dining nooks and crannies around the historic Queen Street East building that Verity Club and George call home. (Many a proposal and many more weddings have occurred within these exposed-brick walls.) Loseto is executive chef at both, part of this go-to address for high-minded cuisine for over a decade. His menus are hyper-seasonal (he's been known to throw arti-choke festivals) and highlight the multiculturalism of this city. From a starter of lobster with avocado brûlée and black quinoa to a main of halibut with curry spätzle and English peas—these are familiar

ingredients reimagined by the chef. Drawing on his Italian upbringing, Loseto's pastas—such as spaghettini with tomato and Asiago—are more straightforward but no less appealing. That said, you can't be in charge of the food at a women's club and not have a great Caesar salad on the menu. Yet Loseto doesn't allow for humdrum greens: his interpretation boasts grilled romaine wedges with daubs of smoky goat cheese mousse, sprouts, tomatoes, olives, and peach. Goodbye goopy dressing and croutons, hello black garlic purée and puffed amaranth! Oh, and then, of course, there are chocolate beignets for dessert.

Butter, for greasing

6 Tbsp cornmeal

6 Tbsp all-purpose flour

¼ cup granulated sugar

¾ tsp baking powder

¼ tsp baking soda

1½ tsp fresh thyme leaves

1 tsp sea salt, plus extra for sprinkling

½ tsp freshly ground black pepper

2 eggs

3 Tbsp unsalted butter, melted

¾ cup sour cream

½ cup fresh corn kernels

2 Tbsp diced bell pepper (colour of your choice)

1 tsp finely diced red chili

 Makes 30

Corn Muffins

Preheat the oven to 400°F. Grease a mini muffin tin and set aside.

In a bowl, combine cornmeal, flour, sugar, baking powder, baking soda, thyme, salt, and pepper. In a separate bowl, combine eggs, butter, sour cream, corn, bell pepper, and chili.

Gently mix dry ingredients into wet ingredients until just combined. Spoon batter into the muffin tins, sprinkle with sea salt, and bake for 5 to 8 minutes, or until cooked through. Place in a basket and serve with salad.

Goat cheese mousse

4 oz goat cheese

½ cup + 2 Tbsp whipping (35%) cream

¼ tsp ground anise seed, toasted

¼ tsp salt

¼ tsp freshly ground black pepper

Black garlic purée

¼ small celery root, peeled and cut into ½-inch cubes

1 head black garlic, peeled (see Tip)

24–30 infornate olives, pitted

1 tsp balsamic vinegar

1 tsp extra-virgin olive oil

½ tsp chopped fresh rosemary

Puffed amaranth

2 cups olive oil

3 Tbsp amaranth seeds

Salt

Salad

1 large romaine heart

Olive oil

Fresh lemon juice

Salt and freshly ground black pepper

2 heirloom beefsteak tomatoes

1 semi-ripe peach

4 mint leaves, finely chopped

1 cup assorted sprouts

7 Tbsp Black Garlic Purée (see here)

Goat Cheese Mousse (see here)

7 Tbsp Puffed Amaranth (see here)

4 Cerignola olives, for garnish

8 cherry or grape tomatoes, for garnish

Black garlic is a caramelized and fermented garlic with a slightly sweet and syrupy taste, commonly used in Asian cuisine. It can be purchased at specialty Asian food stores.

 Serves 4

Romaine, Black Garlic, and Goat Cheese Mousse

Goat cheese mousse Place all ingredients in a bowl and mix together until combined. Set aside.

Black garlic purée Place celery root in a small saucepan of salted water, bring to a boil, and then simmer for 25 minutes, until tender. Drain and then mash.

Place 3½ Tbsp of mashed celery root and the remaining ingredients in a blender and blend until very fine. Set aside.

Puffed amaranth In a saucepan on medium heat, bring olive oil to a boil (temperature should be 350°F). Add amaranth seeds, 1 Tbsp at a time, and shallow-fry for 10 to 30 seconds, until they puff. Strain oil through a fine-mesh sieve and transfer amaranth seeds to a plate lined with paper towel to drain. Season with salt.

Salad Cut romaine vertically into quarters, being careful to keep wedges intact. Season with olive oil, lemon juice, salt, and pepper to taste. In a large frying pan on medium heat, grill lettuce for 1 minute until lightly charred, flip, and grill for another minute. The lettuce should still be cold in the centre.

Cut tomatoes and peach into a variety of shapes, such as 1-inch squares or diamonds, and place in a bowl. Add mint, and olive oil, lemon, salt, and pepper to taste. Toss. Arrange lettuce wedges on each plate and top with a few tomatoes and peaches. Dot with sprouts and black garlic purée and finish with a spoonful of mousse. Sprinkle with puffed amaranth, olives, and cherry tomatoes, and serve. This salad pairs nicely with corn muffins (page 209).

Weslodge

Ben Heaton

THIS TWO-TIERED SPOT on King West is all hunting lodge meets saloon, with wood flooring, cozy nooks, and faux taxidermy lining the walls. Grab a swivel stool at the handsome bar and the barkeep in suspenders will stir up a Gentlemen's Quarterly, while across the way a couple holds hands over a marble-topped table, nibbling on Scotch quail eggs. Meanwhile, a man in a hat sits at a window booth eating an Ontario top sirloin and drinking beer. Everyone has a place here, and chef Ben Heaton turns out big plates of food you want to eat. Deeply burnished fried chicken sided with Brussels sprout slaw, and proper British fries, perfectly crisped on the outside and as fluffy as a pillow on the inside—which makes sense since

Heaton was the chef/owner of the wildly imaginative, British-leaning The Grove restaurant. Even though Weslodge is a modern saloon, this is no roadhouse dive, and there are no shortcuts. A freshly ground burger arrives on a buttery toasted brioche bun, the ketchup is homemade, and even a half portion of the aforementioned chicken is four pieces of crunchy, drippy, sweet and spicy deliciousness. Heaton recently helped launch Icon Legacy Hospitality's sister Weslodge in Dubai, importing an extravagant Grillworks grill— the largest in the Middle East. Another delicious example of "go big or go home."

Brine

21 cups water

¾ cup salt

Seasoned flour

2 cups all-purpose flour

3 Tbsp garlic powder

2½ Tbsp onion powder

1½ Tbsp sweet paprika

1 Tbsp cayenne

1 Tbsp Maldon salt

2 Tbsp freshly ground black pepper

Spicy honey sauce

1 cup + 2 Tbsp honey

¼ cup sherry vinegar

1 Tbsp Tabasco sauce

2 Tbsp Sriracha

Mustard vinaigrette

5 Tbsp Pommery mustard

7 Tbsp fresh lemon juice

1½ Tbsp maple syrup

1 Tbsp lemon zest

½ tsp Maldon salt

¼ tsp freshly ground black pepper

5 Tbsp olive oil

3 Tbsp canola oil

Brussels sprout slaw

4 whole Brussels sprouts, cleaned of outside leaves and thinly sliced

2 Tbsp Mustard Vinaigrette (see here)

Chicken

1 chicken (3 lbs), cut into 8 pieces

Brine (see here)

Assembly

6 cups canola oil

2 cups buttermilk

½ lemon

½ tsp freshly ground black pepper

 Serves 4

Weslodge Fried Chicken

Brine Add water and salt to a large pot and bring to a boil on high heat. Remove from the heat and chill in the fridge until needed.

Seasoned flour Combine all ingredients in a bowl, mix well, and set aside.

Spicy honey sauce In a small saucepan on medium heat, combine all ingredients and bring to a gentle simmer. Set aside to cool, transfer to a sterilized jar, and chill. (It will keep for up to a week.)

Mustard vinaigrette Place all ingredients, except for oils, in a blender and blend until mixed. Gradually add oils and blend until emulsified. Transfer vinaigrette to a bowl and chill in the fridge until needed.

Brussels sprouts slaw Combine ingredients in a bowl and mix well. Reserve for final plating.

Chicken Place chicken in the cold brine and allow to sit between 2 and 4 hours. Remove chicken from brine and pat dry with paper towels.

To assemble Heat canola oil in a deep saucepan on high until the temperature reaches 300°F. Place seasoned flour in a shallow bowl and buttermilk in a separate bowl. Place chicken pieces into flour and coat well. Tap off excess flour and then place into buttermilk. Transfer chicken back into seasoned flour and coat well.

Working in batches, gently lower chicken into hot oil and cook for 8 minutes, until golden brown and crispy and the internal temperature is 165°F. Transfer to a plate lined with paper towels and drain.

Stack chicken on a serving plate, drizzle with honey sauce, and place slaw and lemon on the side. Sprinkle chicken with black pepper and serve immediately.

Pickled corn

6 Tbsp water
6 Tbsp white wine vinegar
3 Tbsp sugar
6 Tbsp frozen corn kernels

Fried shallots

2 shallots, peeled and thinly
   sliced into rings
5 Tbsp cornstarch
4 cups canola oil
½ tsp Maldon salt

Ranch vinaigrette

1½ cups buttermilk
½ cup finely diced celery
⅔ cup chopped fresh dill
⅓ cup white wine vinegar
2 Tbsp finely diced chives
2 Tbsp chopped flat-leaf parsley
1 Tbsp dried dill
1 tsp onion powder
½ tsp garlic powder
¼ tsp paprika
½ tsp Maldon salt
¼ tsp freshly ground black
   pepper
½ cup canola oil

Salad

2 Tbsp red onion, diced
2 heads baby gem lettuce, finely shredded
2 heads endive, finely shredded
1 head radicchio, finely shredded
1 bunch large-leaf spinach, finely shredded
5 Tbsp Ranch Vinaigrette (see here)
¼ tsp Maldon salt
¼ tsp black pepper
¼ cup Pickled Corn (see here)
¼ cup cucumber, peeled and chopped
2 Tbsp red radish, thinly sliced
½ avocado, chopped
3 Tbsp crumbled feta
1 tsp finely chopped chives
20 Fried Shallots (see here)
2 Tbsp celery leaves
½ tsp lemon zest
Extra-virgin olive oil, for drizzling
Freshly ground black pepper

 Serves 2

Weslodge Chop Salad

Pickled corn In a small saucepan on medium heat, combine water and vinegar, bring to a simmer, and add sugar. Stir until sugar has dissolved. Place corn in a small bowl, add pickling liquid, and set aside for 2 hours. (It'll keep for 2 weeks in the fridge.)

Fried shallots In a bowl, combine shallots and cornstarch and mix well until shallots are completely coated. Shake off any excess corn-starch. Heat canola oil in a deep saucepan on high, until the temperature reaches 275°F. Fry shallot rings for 2 minutes, or until golden brown. Using a slotted spoon, transfer shallots to a plate lined with paper towels. Season with salt and reserve.

Ranch vinaigrette Combine all ingredients except canola oil in a blender and purée until smooth. Gradually add oil and blend until emulsi-fied. Check seasoning and adjust, if necessary.

Salad Bring a small saucepan of water to a boil on medium heat, add red onions, and blanch for 1 minute. Drain and transfer to a bowl of ice water. Drain when cool, pat dry with paper towel, and set aside.

In a large bowl, combine lettuce, endive, radic-chio, and spinach and toss well, then add vinai-grette and massage the dressing into the greens. Season with salt and pepper.

Pile salad in 2 serving bowls and top with corn, cucumber, radish, red onion, and avocado. Sprinkle with feta and chives and garnish with fried shallots, celery leaves, and lemon zest. Drizzle with olive oil and finish with freshly ground black pepper.

The Wickson Social

Andrew Carter

AS YOU SPY A PARADE of young women with lap dogs and men in tracksuits streaming from the luxury St. Joseph Street condo above, you don't expect the warm room and British-leaning menu to make you feel so cared for. Yet this third restaurant from co-owners chef Andrew Carter and Jamieson Kerr (The Oxley and The Queen and Beaver) does just that. At the base of the new glassy structure sits architect Frank Wickson's gothic warehouse, now reimagined into a colourful hub for cocktails, brunch, lunch, and dinner. Order a cocktail (I recommend a Kerfuffle) and tuck into some globally inspired shared plates, then mains like the cep-tarragon risotto with dry-cured venison. "Classics such as risotto can be daunting, but this one is somewhat forgiving due to the nature of the sauce," says Carter. As for his trio of ice cream recipes, "Each has its own story of how it came into existence." The whiskey-gingerbread was born in the U.K.'s Lake District, the chocolate has an origin story based in Switzerland, and the divisive Stilton and wild cherry is one for the ages. Stop by the restaurant and ask Chef Carter for his ice cream stories. I'm sure he'll be more than happy to oblige.

FACING: Ice Cream Trio: Whiskey Gingerbread, Chocolate, and Stilton and Wild Cherry

Whiskey gingerbread ice cream

1½ cups superfine sugar

6 egg yolks

4 Tbsp whiskey

3 cups whipping (35%) cream

3 cups crumbled gingerbread

Pinch of salt

Chocolate ice cream

10 egg yolks

1¼ cups superfine sugar

½ cup cocoa powder

3 cups whipping (35%) cream

1 cup 2% milk

1 cup chopped dark chocolate

 Serves 6

Ice Cream Trio: Whiskey Gingerbread, Chocolate, and Stilton and Wild Cherry

Whiskey gingerbread ice cream Bring a large pot of water to a simmer on medium heat. In a large metal bowl, combine sugar, egg yolks, and whiskey and whisk over the pot of water for 8 minutes, until ribbons form when mixture is dropped from a spoon. Set aside.

In a separate bowl, whisk cream until it reaches the ribbon stage, then fold into the sugar-and-egg mixture. Fold in gingerbread and salt. Pour mixture into desired shallow storage container and place in the freezer overnight.

Chocolate ice cream In a large bowl, combine egg yolks and sugar and whisk for 4 minutes, or until pale. Sift in cocoa powder and mix until slightly thickened. Set aside.

In a heavy-bottomed saucepan on medium heat, combine cream and milk and bring to a boil, stirring constantly. Remove from the heat. Add 1 cup of cream mixture to egg mixture and stir well. (Adding the hot mixture gradually prevents the eggs from scrambling.) Gradually add the remainder of cream mixture, stirring continuously, until well mixed. Stir in chocolate.

Pour mixture through a fine-mesh strainer and refrigerate for 1 to 2 hours, until cool. Pour cooled mixture into an ice-cream maker and freeze according to the manufacturer's instructions. Remove from the freezer about 10 minutes before serving.

Stilton and wild cherry ice cream
10 egg yolks
1¼ cups superfine sugar
4 cups whipping (35%) cream
4 cups 2% milk
½ vanilla bean
½ cup Amarena cherries, halved
1 cup crumbled Stilton, crumbled into
   ½-inch pieces

Stilton and wild cherry ice cream Bring a large pot of water to a simmer on medium heat. In a large bowl, combine egg yolks and sugar and whisk for 4 minutes, or until pale.

Combine the milk and cream in a heavy-bottomed saucepan. With a sharp paring knife, split the vanilla bean lengthwise and scrape out the seeds, then add seeds and pod to the milk-and-cream mixture. On a medium heat, slowly bring the mixture to a boil.

Add 1 cup of cream mixture to egg mixture and stir well. (Adding the hot mixture gradually prevents the eggs from scrambling.) Gradually add the remainder of cream mixture, stirring continuously, until well mixed. Place bowl on top of a pan of simmering water to cook the custard, stirring continuously with a wooden spoon until it evenly coats the back of the spoon.

Remove from heat and pour through a fine-mesh strainer. Refrigerate for 1 to 2 hours, until cool. Pour cooled mixture into an ice-cream maker, and freeze according to the manufacturer's instructions. Once frozen, fold in the Stilton and cherries, then place in the freezer overnight.

Herb butter
1 cup unsalted butter, softened
2 Tbsp chopped fresh tarragon
2 Tbsp chopped chives
2 Tbsp chopped flat-leaf parsley

Red wine sauce
2 Tbsp unsalted butter
6 shallots, sliced
3 cloves garlic, finely chopped
2 bay leaves
½ bunch fresh thyme, tied in
   a bundle with twine
2 cups red wine
2 cups beef stock

Cep cream
2 cups dried cep mushrooms (porcini)
4 cups boiling water
2 Tbsp unsalted butter
6 shallots, sliced
2 cloves garlic, minced
3 bay leaves
½ bunch fresh thyme, tied in a bundle
   with twine
1 Tbsp dried tarragon
½ cup Noilly Prat white vermouth
Salt and white pepper, to taste
2 cups Red Wine Sauce (see here) or
   beef stock
4 cups whipping (35%) cream

 Serves 4

Cep-Tarragon Risotto with Dry-Cured Venison

Herb butter Combine all ingredients in a food processor and process until blended. Scrape butter out onto a sheet of plastic wrap. Mould into a log and wrap tightly in the plastic. Roll wrapped butter back and forth on the counter to create a smooth, round log. Refrigerate until ready to use. (For longer storage, wrap butter log in a piece of aluminum foil, label, and freeze. It will keep for several months.)

Red wine sauce In a heavy-bottomed frying pan on medium heat, melt butter. Add shallots, garlic, bay leaves, and thyme and sauté for 4 to 5 minutes, until translucent. Add wine, increase heat to medium-high, and cook for another 6 minutes, until liquid is reduced by two-thirds. Add stock and cook for another 5 minutes, until liquid is reduced to 2 cups. Pour sauce through a fine-mesh strainer and set aside.

Cep cream Wash dried ceps under cold running water for 5 minutes. Place in a medium bowl, add boiling water, cover, and let stand for 20 minutes.

Meanwhile, melt butter in a heavy-bottomed saucepan on medium heat. Add shallots, garlic, bay leaves, thyme, and tarragon and sauté for 4 to 5 minutes, until shallots are translucent.

Drain ceps and add to shallot mixture, cooking for another 4 minutes, slightly covered, until mushrooms are soft. Reduce heat to low and carefully add vermouth. (If the pan is too hot, mixture may ignite due to the high alcohol content.) Cook for another 5 minutes, until most of the liquid has evaporated. Season with salt and pepper, then add red wine sauce (or beef stock). Bring to a simmer over medium heat and cook for 4 minutes, until liquid is reduced by a third. Stir in cream, bring back to a simmer, and cook for another 3 minutes, until liquid is reduced by a quarter. Pour sauce through a fine-mesh strainer and set aside. (Makes about 2½ cups.)

Risotto

2 Tbsp unsalted butter

3 shallots, finely chopped

1 clove garlic, finely chopped

1 bay leaf

½ bunch fresh thyme, tied in a bundle with twine

4 cups Arborio rice

½ Tbsp salt, plus extra to taste

12 cups cold water, divided

Assembly

7 oz home-cured venison shoulder or store-bought bresaola, thinly sliced

2 Tbsp truffle oil or 4 Tbsp good-quality extra-virgin olive oil, for drizzling

Risotto In a heavy-bottomed frying pan on low heat, melt butter. Add shallots, garlic, bay leaf, and thyme and sauté for 4 minutes, or until translucent. Stir in rice, mix until well coated in the liquid, and cook for 5 minutes. Add salt and 1 cup of water, increase heat to medium, and stir continuously until most of the liquid has been absorbed. Continue to add water, 1 cup at a time, and repeat the process for 15 to 20 minutes, until rice is al dente. Transfer rice onto a parchment-lined baking sheet and set aside.

To assemble Set the oven to the warming function or preheat to 100°F (or the lowest temperature possible). Once the oven reaches the desired temperature, turn off the heat and place 4 serving dishes or bowls on the rack.

To a heavy-bottomed frying pan on medium heat, add 6 cups risotto, stir in cep cream, and heat, stirring occasionally, until warmed through. Add 2 Tbsp herb butter and stir to finish. Remove warmed dishes or bowls from the oven, portion out the rice, and top with venison or bresaola. Drizzle with truffle oil or olive oil and serve immediately.

Zucca Trattoria

Andrew Milne-Allan

A RESTAURANT THAT GRILLS whole branzino and serves it with nothing but a bottle of olive oil and a bowl of grey sea salt is a place for me. And that place is Zucca. Since 1996, chef Andrew Milne-Allan's midtown institution has been serving hyper-seasonal food, simply and impeccably—with service to match. Prior to Zucca, he cheffed at Toronto's Mediterranean-focused The Parrot in the 1970s and launched Trattoria Giancarlo in the 1980s. There was a culinary optimism at the time, and his restaurants were big steps forward for the city. The room at Zucca fades into the background as vibrant plates arrive: burrata-stuffed squash blossoms, and grilled country bread with sweet fresh figs, truffled pecorino, and rosemary oil. You cannot leave without ordering at least one fish and one pasta dish for the table, though the *contorni*,

mostly vegetable side dishes, are no afterthought. On this night, the *tortino*—a gratin of fresh arti-chokes and potato with herbs, caciocavallo, and breadcrumbs—almost causes a fork fight. Many of the pastas were born in small towns in Italy, be it spaghetti all'Amatriciana from Amatrice or the maccheroni sauced with a saffron-infused rock-fish ragu. Says Chef Milne-Allan of his maccheroni recipe: "This is a handmade Sicilian pasta that can be made without machinery, although a stand mixer will make life a little easier." Perfection is not necessarily the goal, and, in fact, a little irregularity is key. "It helps the sauce cling to the pasta," he says. "The texture in the mouth reminds you that it's handmade."

FACING: Maccheroni with Rockfish Ragu, Saffron, Raisins, and Pinenuts

Pasta

1 cup all-purpose flour

2½ cups semolina flour

½ tsp salt

2 tsp extra-virgin olive oil

¾ cup warm water

Rockfish ragu

Good pinch of saffron

2 Tbsp sultana raisins

1 whole rockfish (1½–2 lbs), cleaned, scaled, and filleted, and head and frame roughly chopped

¼ cup extra-virgin olive oil, divided

½ onion, diced

½ carrot, diced

1 rib celery, diced

1 bay leaf

1½ tsp salt, divided

2 cloves garlic, crushed

1 anchovy fillet

3 sprigs fresh marjoram, tied in a bundle with string

½ cup dry white wine

1 can (14 oz) plum tomatoes, chopped

2 cups water

6–8 sprigs flat-leaf parsley, chopped

¼ cup toasted pine nuts

 Serves 4–6

Maccheroni with Rockfish Ragu, Saffron, Raisins, and Pinenuts

Pasta Mix flours, salt, and oil together in the bowl of a stand mixer. Attach a dough hook and set on medium. Gradually add water until dough comes together. (If it's too dry, add more water sparingly as necessary.) Knead for 5 minutes. Turn dough out onto a board and knead by hand for 5 minutes, or until dough feels smooth and silky to the touch. Cover with plastic wrap and leave to rest for 30 minutes.

Unwrap dough and divide into 5 pieces. On a wooden work surface, roll each piece into a long cylinder, about ⅜ inch in diameter (or the thickness of a pencil). Line cylinders up and cut across into 2½-inch lengths. Working with one piece at a time, press a skewer lengthwise into the middle of the dough. Roll the skewer back and forth vigorously with your palm until dough wraps around the skewer. Continue to roll as dough lengthens, adding your other hand until dough approaches the end of the skewer and is about 7 inches in length. Grip pasta with one hand and, with a sharp twist, remove the skewer with the other. Lay pasta on a floured sheet to dry for an hour or two. Repeat with remaining pieces.

Rockfish ragu Place saffron and ¼ cup warm water in a small bowl and set aside to steep. Place sultanas in a bowl of warm water and soak for 20 minutes. Squeeze dry.

Using tweezers, remove any pin bones from rockfish fillets. Chop into ½-inch cubes, place in a bowl, and refrigerate until needed.

Heat 2 Tbsp olive oil in a small frying pan on medium-low and add onions, carrots, celery, bay leaf, and a ¼ tsp salt. Stir frequently with a wooden spoon and cook for 25 minutes, or until soft and fragrant. (Do not brown.) Remove from the heat and set aside.

In a pan large enough to comfortably hold the fish head and bones, heat the remaining 2 Tbsp of olive oil on medium-low. Add garlic and cook for 3 minutes, or until golden. Add anchovy, marjoram, and fish head and bones. Using a rubber spatula, scrape in softened vegetables. Shake the pan back and forth to settle everything into the flavoured oil.

Increase the heat to medium and add white wine. Let mixture bubble and reduce for 1 to 2 minutes. Add tomatoes, the remaining 1¼ tsp salt, and water. Bring to a vigorous boil. Reduce heat to medium, cover, and simmer for 25 minutes. Discard marjoram and bay leaf.

Set a food mill fitted with a medium blade over a container that will hold all the sauce. Using tongs, transfer the fish head and bones to the mill. Moisten with a ladle or two of sauce. Use a constant forward and reverse motion to loosen the bones as you go. Continue to pass remaining sauce through the mill. Discard the bones.

Return sauce to the pan. Check seasoning and adjust to taste. Add diced fish, sultanas, and saffron with its liquid. Simmer briefly until fish is cooked, 5 minutes or so. Set aside.

Bring a large pot of salted water to a boil. Drop in pasta and cook for 4 to 5 minutes, until pasta is tender but still has a bite. (The cooking time will depend on how long you left the pasta to dry. If you are using a dry imported pasta, follow the package instructions.) Transfer cooked pasta to the pan with the sauce, which you can reheat if necessary. Heat together for a minute or so, stirring pasta gently. Add parsley.

Transfer to a large, warm serving bowl or individual plates. Scatter with toasted pine nuts and enjoy.

24 asparagus spears (about 1½ lbs)

2–3 large, firm white mushrooms, trimmed

Salt

¼ lemon

½ cup extra-virgin olive oil, divided

1 large bunch arugula, washed and dried

1 cup grated Parmigiano-Reggiano

 Serves 4

Warm Asparagus and Mushroom Salad

Snap the ends off asparagus, then peel the base of the stalks with a vegetable peeler. Trim to an even length. Wash well and use kitchen string to tie them into 2 bunches.

Preheat the oven to 500°F. Wipe mushrooms clean with a damp cloth. Slice thinly using a knife or mandoline. Allow 5 to 6 slices for each portion of salad. Lay slices close together on a baking sheet without overlapping and season lightly with salt. Squeeze lemon into a small bowl, add 2 Tbsp water and 1 Tbsp olive oil, and whisk together. Pour over mushrooms and set aside.

In a high-sided pot on high heat, bring a few inches of water to a boil. (Alternatively, use an asparagus steamer.) Add asparagus upright and steam, covered, for 4 to 5 minutes, until tender but still firm. Reserve the cooking water.

Transfer asparagus to a large bowl and cut the strings. Season with salt, then add a small ladle of cooking water and remaining olive oil. Allow to cool slightly.

Meanwhile, lay arugula on 4 plates. Place the baking sheet of mushrooms in the oven for 1 to 2 minutes, just long enough for mushrooms to give off a little steam. Remove the baking sheet from the oven and arrange mushroom slices on each plate of arugula in a random pattern. Pour any juices from the mushrooms over the salads.

Gently toss asparagus in the bowl and add Parmigiano-Reggiano in small amounts, creating a creamy sauce. Add a little more cooking water if necessary. Lay asparagus spears over mushrooms and arugula in a basket-weave fashion, alternating tops and tails. Pour remaining sauce over top and serve.

Metric Conversion Chart

Volume

Imperial	Metric
⅛ tsp	0.5 mL
¼ tsp	1 mL
½ tsp	2.5 mL
¾ tsp	4 mL
1 tsp	5 mL
½ Tbsp	8 mL
1 Tbsp	15 mL
1½ Tbsp	23 mL
2 Tbsp	30 mL
¼ cup	60 mL
⅓ cup	80 mL
½ cup	125 mL
⅔ cup	165 mL
¾ cup	185 mL
1 cup	250 mL
1¼ cups	310 mL
1⅓ cups	330 mL
1½ cups	375 mL
1⅔ cups	415 mL
1¾ cups	435 mL
2 cups	500 mL
2¼ cups	560 mL
2⅓ cups	580 mL
2½ cups	625 mL
2¾ cups	690 mL
3 cups	750 mL
4 cups / 1 qt	1 L
5 cups	1.25 L
6 cups	1.5 L
7 cups	1.75 L
8 cups	2 L

Weight

Imperial	Metric
½ oz	15 g
1 oz	30 g
2 oz	60 g
3 oz	85 g
4 oz (¼ lb)	115 g
5 oz	140 g
6 oz	170 g
7 oz	200 g
8 oz (½ lb)	225 g
9 oz	255 g
10 oz	285 g
11 oz	310 g
12 oz (¾ lb)	340 g
13 oz	370 g
14 oz	400 g
15 oz	425 g
16 oz (1 lb)	450 g
1¼ lb	570 g
1½ lb	670 g
2 lb	900 g
3 lb	1.4 kg
4 lb	1.8 kg
5 lb	2.3 kg
6 lb	2.7 kg

Linear

Imperial	Metric
⅛ inch	3 mm
¼ inch	6 mm
½ inch	12 mm
¾ inch	2 cm
1 inch	2.5 cm
1¼ inches	3 cm
1½ inches	3.5 cm
1¾ inches	4.5 cm
2 inches	5 cm
2½ inches	6.5 cm
3 inches	7.5 cm
4 inches	10 cm
5 inches	12.5 cm
6 inches	15 cm
7 inches	18 cm
10 inches	25 cm
12 inches (1 foot)	30 cm
13 inches	33 cm
16 inches	41 cm
18 inches	46 cm
24 inches (2 feet)	60 cm
28 inches	70 cm
30 inches	75 cm
6 feet	1.8 m

Liquid measures (for alcohol)

Imperial	Metric
1 fl oz	30 mL
2 fl oz	60 mL
3 fl oz	90 mL
4 fl oz	120 mL

Cans and Jars

Imperial	Metric	
6 oz	170 g	180 mL
7 oz	198 g	200 mL
14 oz	397 g	398 mL
28 oz	794 g	796 mL

Baking Pans

Imperial	Metric
5 × 9-inch loaf pan	2 L loaf pan
9 × 13-inch cake pan	4 L cake pan
11 × 17-inch baking sheet	30 × 45-cm baking sheet

Oven temperature

Imperial	Metric
200°F	95°C
250°F	120°C
275°F	135°C
300°F	150°C
325°F	160°C
350°F	180°C
375°F	190°C
400°F	200°C
425°F	220°C
450°F	230°C

Temperature

Imperial	Metric
90°F	32°C
120°F	49°C
125°F	52°C
130°F	54°C
140°F	60°C
150°F	66°C
155°F	68°C
160°F	71°C
165°F	74°C
170°F	77°C
175°F	80°C
180°F	82°C
190°F	88°C
200°F	93°C
240°F	116°C
250°F	121°C
300°F	149°C
325°F	163°C
350°F	177°C
360°F	182°C
375°F	191°C

Acknowledgements

Thank you!

I'd like to thank the chefs and makers who shared their stories and recipes in this book. *Toronto Eats* may be the second in a series, but you've helped create a cookbook that is wholly original. Our city is a delicate potpourri of cultures, making for an exciting culinary journey. You all have illustrated this magically.

Thank you to the Figure 1 team, including Chris Labonté, Richard Nadeau, Jessica Sullivan (our ace book designer), Jennifer Smith, Michelle Meade, and Lara Smith. You make creating cookbooks a wonderful experience, where the best can be expressed in the most beautiful way imaginable.

To that end, Ryan Szulc, your photographic skills and vision for this project surpassed my wildest expectations. You, along with the amazing prop stylist Madeleine Johari, have created another singular look—a dream team if ever there was one. I'd like to extend my gratitude to Ryan's studio crew, who made a very complicated shoot (relatively) stress-free.

And finally, much love and gratitude to my family and friends for being ever-encouraging, gleefully enthusiastic, and always hungry for more.

Index

burnt honey and saffron aioli, 23

BUTTER. *See also* brown butter
    cashew, 29
    cashew-pandan, 8
    herb, 220
    honey herb and spice, *4, 6*
    iwa nori, 137
buttercream, 71

CABBAGE. *See also* Brussels sprout(s);
    kale
    in okonomiyaki, 111
    Savoy, in choucroute garnie, 191
    in spicy citrus slaw, 106
Caesar salad, avocado kale, 53
CAKES
    celebration cake, 70
    "cheesecake" with strawberry
      sauce, 125
caramelized bananas, 185
caramel sauce, salted honey and
    rosemary, 82
"carbonara," parsnip tagliatelle, 206
carpaccio, hearts of palm, 58–59
carrots, in Thai root vegetable salad, 29
cashew butter, 29
cashew-dill ricotta, 127
cashew-pandan mousse, passion
    fruit purée, and lime tuile, 8–9
cashews, in "cheesecake" filling, 125
celebration cake, 70–71
cep cream, 220
cep-tarragon risotto with dry-cured
    venison, 220–21
"Chalet" sauce, 103
chanterelles, with zucchini and prawn
    salad, 145
charred onion, cured trout grilled over
    cedar and, 40
cheeks, Barolo-braised, 167
CHEESE
    Fontina, in cheesy polenta, 167
    goat cheese mousse, 211
    mortadella, in muffuletta, 64
    mozzarella, in Margherita
      pizza, 165
    Parmesan eggplant sandwich, 133
    Parmesan garlic bread, 105
    PARMIGIANO-REGGIANO
      in Apocalypse Cow pizza, 135
      in cheesy polenta, 167
      in meatballs, 135
    pecorino, tagliatelle with, 31
    pecorino focaccia bianca, 37
    Piave, in arugula salad, 163
    provolone, in muffuletta, 64

ricotta, cashew-dill, 127
ricotta polenta, 194
ricotta with truffle honey, 95
sheep's milk, slow-cooked chicken
    with, 98
Stilton and wild cherry ice cream,
    216, 219
"cheesecake" with strawberry
    sauce, 125
cheesy polenta, Barolo-braised beef
    cheeks with, 167
CHERRIES
    Amarena, in Stilton and wild
      cherry ice cream, *216, 219*
    Morello, in dark chocolate cherry
      tart with white chocolate
      ganache, *78, 80–81*
CHICKEN
    fried, Weslodge, 213
    lemongrass, 193
    in paella del Carmen, 48
    slow-cooked, 98
    smoked, with "Chalet" sauce, 103
chicken liver and foie gras
    mousse, 152
chicken pad Thai, 157, *157*
chicken sandwich, 51
chicken satay skewers, 143, *143*
chickpeas, in hearts of palm carpac-
    cio, 58–59
chili, turkey, with cornbread croutons
    and chive sour cream, 85
chili crab, Mumbai, 114
CHILI(ES). *See also* peppers
    Anaheim, in chili-lime dressing, 29
    ancho, dried, in pato con mole, 47
    BIRD'S-EYE
      in chili oil, 145
      in corn pakoras, 113
      in Mumbai chili crab, 114
      in picante Pasini, 200
    chipotle, dried, in pato con mole, 47
    dried, in peanut sauce, 143
    finger, red, in muffuletta, 64
    grapefruit syrup, 200
    habanero, in muffuletta, 64
    -lime dressing, 29
    morito, dried, in pato con mole, 47
    oil, in zucchini and prawn
      salad, 145
    poblano, in slow-cooked
      chicken, 98
    RED
      in bay scallop and shrimp
        balls, 160
      in corn muffins, 209

in lamb shank baklava, 22
roasted, in grilled mackerel
    with marinated peppers, 199
in saffron tomato sauce, 93
in spinach curry, 113
serrano, in tomato salsa, 68
Thai, dried, in chicken satay, 143
Chinese yam (Shan Yao), 111
chipotle chili, dried, in pato con
    mole, 47
chips, spiced kale, 138
chive sour cream, turkey chili
    with, 85
CHOCOLATE
    chocolate chip cookie squares, 181
    chocolate ice cream, *216*, 218
    chocolate tart dough, 81
    dark chocolate cherry tart with
      white chocolate ganache, *78,
      80–81*
    Pusateri's chocolate chip banana
      bread, 169
    Sierra's insanely awesome
      brownies, 90, *90*
    whipped white chocolate
      ganache, 186
chorizo sausage, in paella del
    Carmen, 48
choucroute garnie, 191
choux pastry, 184
CHOWDER
    East Coast mussel haddock, 129
    Honest Weight mussel and
      clam, 109
chutney, lemongrass chicken
    and, 193
cider, pork in, 189
cinnamon sugar, 179
citrus-roasted potatoes, *148*, 150
citrus slaw, spicy, 106
CLAMS
    in Honest Weight chowder, 109
    in paella del Carmen, 48
classic sour cream doughnuts, 179
coconut and graham crust, for
    lime tart, 97
COD
    in ackee 'n' saltfish cakes, 159
    in açorda de bacalhau, 101
    in Fogo Island fish tacos, 106
    in okonomiyaki, 111
coffee, brewed cold, 89, *90*
cold brew, 89, *90*
coleslaw. *See* slaw
confit egg yolk, wood nettle spätzle
    and, 39

About
the Author
Amy Rosen

AMY ROSEN is an award-winning journalist and cookbook author who writes regularly for publications such as *enRoute*, *Food & Wine*, and *Food & Drink*. She is the former food editor at *Chatelaine* and *House & Home*, has been a columnist for the *Globe and Mail* and *National Post*, and has been nominated for a James Beard Award. Her latest adventure is a venture: Amy launched Rosen's Cinnamon Buns in the autumn of 2016, and the city is loving her buns!